THE GREATEST
OF THEM ALL

THE LEGEND OF BOBBY JONES

Published by:
The American Golfer, Inc.
135 East Putnam Avenue
Greenwich, CT 06830
(203) 862-9720
FAX (203) 862-9724

Distribution to the golf trade by:
The Booklegger
13100 Grass Valley Avenue
Grass Valley, CA 95945
(916) 272-1556

Distribution to the book trade by:
Login Publishers Consortium
1436 W. Randolph Street
Chicago, IL 60607
(312) 413-7020

Design by:
NSI Design Group, Inc.
37 W. 17th Street
New York, NY 10011
(212) 206-9090

Film and separations by:
Creative Graphic Services Corp.
56 Budney Road
Newington, CT 06111
(860) 247-3737

Graphics International Inc.
1930 Monroe Drive
Atlanta, GA 30324
(404) 873-5271

Printed by Amilcare Pizzi, Milan, Italy

ACKNOWLEDGMENTS

First and foremost, we would like to thank the Jones family for their cooperation and assistance in the production of this book. We would also like to formally recognize the efforts of Marty Elgison and Gene Branch of the law firm of Alston and Bird, Bob Jones' law firm, without whose assistance this book could not have been produced.

Needless to say, we would also like to thank our contributing essayists for their fine efforts: Alistair Cooke, Dave Anderson, Ben Crenshaw, Peter Dobereiner, Nick Seitz and Larry Dorman. Thanks also to Sal Johnson for the thorough research effort in compiling the detailed Appendix of Bob Jones' golf achievements. And thanks to Ray Kinstler for the fine original oil painting of Bob Jones on the dust jacket.

A very special thanks to Dr. Richard Gordin, whose PhD thesis in 1967 was on Bob Jones. Both the research contained in his thesis and his input were invaluable in the production of this book.

Several organizations and individuals were responsible for providing the original photographs accompanying these pages; specifically Linda Matthews, Beverly Allen and Kathy Knox of the Special Collections Department of the R.W. Woodruff Library at Emory University, Karen Bednarski, Andy Much, Nancy Stulack and Patty Moran of the United States Golf Association, Saundra Sheffer and Marge Dewy of the Ralph W. Miller Golf Library, Rick Beard, Lynn Watson-Powers and Ted Ryan of the Atlanta History Center, Chris Borders, Donna Hand, and the Board of Directors of the Atlanta Athletic Club, Dominic Young of *The* (London) *Times*, The Bettmann Archive, the Associated Press, the University of St. Andrews Picture Collection, Anne Williams of Frank Christian Studios, Tom Nieporte of the Winged Foot Golf Club, World Wide Photos of Palm Beach and Carolyn Cole of the Los Angeles Public Library.

We would also like to acknowledge Charlie Yates, Mr. Jones' dear friend, for his special insights and assistance.

Thanks also to those who provided first hand accounts of Mr. Jones for this book: Charlie Seaver, Harry Cooper, Paul Runyon, Bill Hyndman, Bill Campbell and Ely Callaway.

A special thanks too to the Augusta National Golf Club, and especially Barbara and Dave Spencer, as well as Kathryn Murphy, the always helpful and gracious secretary of the Masters, for their advice, encouragement and assistance.

Also, we would like to single out Nancy Koch of NSI Design for the superb design and art direction, Des Tolhurst for his most knowledgeable editorial assistance and Creative Graphics for the magnificent film work. In addition, we would also like to acknowledge the fine efforts of Graphics International for the Atlanta portion of the film work.

In addition, our thanks to Michael Bonallack of the R&A and David Begg, of David Begg Sports Promotions in the UK.

A special thanks also to Scott Sayers for his editorial and organizational support and to Bruce Smith for his help and encouragement.

Last, and certainly not least, I would like to single out my most able assistant, Alyssa Rebosio for her invaluable contributions, the least of which has been keeping straight the myriad details involved in a production of this size.

Again our sincerest thanks to all who contributed so mightily.

ISBN 1-1-888531-00-2: $60.00

For Herb Wind, the Bob Jones of golf writers.

THE GREATEST OF THEM ALL

THE LEGEND OF BOBBY JONES

By Martin Davis

Classic Photography of the Incomparable Bobby Jones ■ **Foreword By Alistair Cooke** ■ **Essays by Dave Anderson, Ben Crenshaw, Peter Dobereiner, Nick Seitz, and Larry Dorman** ■ **Original Reporting by Bernard Darwin, O.B. Keeler and Grantland Rice**

The American Golfer, Inc. ● 135 East Putnam Avennue ● Greenwich, CT 06830 ● 203-862-9724; (fax) 203-862-9724

TABLE OF CONTENTS

Photography and Commentary:

CHAMPION OF CHAMPIONS

BY MARTIN DAVIS

One of the most enduring and enjoyable aspects in sports is trying to determine who is the all-time best. Was Babe Ruth the greatest baseball player of all time or was it Hank Aaron? In tennis, was it Bill Tilden, Rod Laver or John McEnroe? In basketball who was the best — was it Bill Russell, Wilt Chamberlin or Kareem Abdul Jabbar? Or is it Michael Jordan? In each sport the debate, it seems, is never-ending.

Of course, golf is not immune to these discussions. What it invariably comes down to are the three great champions of the modern era: Bobby Jones — the winner of 13 major championships and the only one to ever carry- off the Grand Slam of all four majors in one year, Ben Hogan — the winner of nine majors, including three in one year, and Jack Nicklaus — the winner of more majors, 20, than anyone else.

Each of these great golfers clearly dominated his era more completely than anyone else. And each had stiff competition in his own time: Jones was pitted against Walter Hagen and Gene Sarazen; Hogan primarily against Sam Snead, but also against Jimmy Demaret and Byron Nelson; and Nicklaus against Arnold Palmer, Gary Player, Lee Trevino and Tom Watson.

It seems reasonable then, that a logical method of determining who, among these great champions, was the best is to ascertain who was more dominant within their era than the others. In this way we are able to compare players of different eras, playing under vastly different conditions with quite different equipment.

By his record, it is abundantly clear that Jones dominated his competitors more completely than anyone else has done over a significant period of time.

Just consider Jones' record in the major tournaments: from his first championship as a 14 year-old phenom in the 1916 U.S. Amateur to his retirement in 1930, Bob Jones played in 31 majors. He won 13 of them and finished second in four. Amazingly, if one analyzes just the period of time from when he won his first championship in 1923 at the age of 21, until the time he retired at 28 in 1930, Bob Jones either won or finished second better than 80 percent of the time! And during that period only once did Hagen or Sarazen finish ahead of him.

But Bob Jones was much more than perhaps the greatest of golfers. Was he perfect? Certainly not. Yet there was more than enough substance in his character to make him a role model for today: his educational achievements, his innate modesty, his sense of fair play, his competitive zeal, and the manner in which he balanced the various facets of his life. These are attributes truly worthy of emulation.

Pat Ward-Thomas, the wonderful British golf writer, observed "Down the years people have wondered whether Jones was the greatest of all golfers. Comparison is invidious, for no man can do more than win and Jones won more often within a given period than anyone else has ever done. … in his time, Jones was supreme, at match and medal play, to a greater extent than Hogan or Nicklaus have been in theirs."

We hope you enjoy reading about Bob Jones.

WHAT HAVE WE LEFT FOR BOBBY JONES?

BY ALISTAIR COOKE

On the centennial of the birth of Mr. Justice Holmes, I was asked to write a commemorative piece for a liberal weekly. By that time, his reputation as a liberal hero was as secure as Jane Austen's new reputation as a pioneer feminist, an elevation that, if she were within earshot, would — as she might say — "vastly astound" her. Holmes had been so exhaustively written about, so firmly established as The Great Dissenter, that there seemed very little to say about him. I accordingly said very little and summed it all up in the title of the piece: "What Have We Left For Mr. Justice Holmes?" It took many years, and the leisure to look him over freed from his obituary pigeon hole, to make the alarming discovery that the cases in which he voted with the conservative majority as against it were in the ratio of eight or ten to one; and that two notable scholars succeeded each other in spending years preparing his biography only to abandon it to a third man who saw what they had seen in Holmes, but one who also had the courage to say it out loud: that Holmes's political philosophy was (his concern for free speech apart) as fine an intellectual approximation to fascism as you would care to find among the savants of the Western world.

I have come to a similar hurdle with Robert Tyre Jones, Jr. though one nothing like so formidable or alarming. I don't suppose any other athletic hero, certainly no one in golf, has been written about so often and with so much reverence. The same admirable anecdotes are repeated whenever his name is mentioned: his debunking of the teaching clichés ("never up, never in"); his famous put down by Harry Vardon ("did you ever see a worse shot than that?"); his identifying the enemy as "Old Man Par"; his calling a two-stroke penalty on himself to lose a championship ("you might as well praise a man for not robbing a bank"). And on and on. Anyone reading this book, certainly anyone getting it for review, has heard these stories a hundred times and must have concluded long ago that fresh anecdotes about Jones are as few and far between as new funny golf stories. This must be, then, a small memoir of a short friendship in the last years of his life and what I gleaned about him and his character.

In the summer of 1965, when I had been for nearly 20 years the chief American correspondent, of *The* (then *Manchester*) *Guardian,* our golf correspondent, Pat Ward-Thomas, for some reason or other was unable to cover the U.S. Open championship, which was being held, I believe for the first time, at Creve Coeur in St. Louis. I filled in for him and my last day's dispatch eventually appeared in the *Guardian's* annual anthology of the paper's writing. Somehow, a copy of it got to Jones. He wrote me a letter saying, as I recall, he was unaware that "golf was another string to your bow." Why he should have known anything at all about my "bow" was news to me. But he mentioned that he had been a regular viewer of "Omnibus", a 90-minute network television pot-pourri of drama, science, politics, history, ballet, and God knows what, which I hosted in the 1950's. Jones' letter was, of course, highly flattering to me, especially since this was the first piece I had ever written about golf. I had taken up the game only one year before, at an advanced age (in my mid-fifties — hopeless, I know); but, being a journalist, I started to write about it, just as when you run into a man who is an expert on the manufacture of heels for ladies' shoes — as was a man I met in Rainelle, W. Virginia — you write about *him*.

> HIS PREFERENCE WAS FOR ABE MITCHELL'S "THE PLAYER SHOULD MOVE FREELY BENEATH HIMSELF."

There was another short exchange or two, in one of which Jones characteristically started a letter; "Dear Alistair (don't you think we ought to put an end to this minuet of Mr. Jones and Mr. Cooke?)" and went on to ask me to be sure to call on him whenever I was down in Augusta or Atlanta. Which I did, most often in the company of Ward-Thomas.

My first impression was the shock of seeing the extent of his disability, the fine strong hands, twisted like the branches of a cypress, gamely clutching a tumbler or one of his perpetual cigarettes in a holder. His face was more ravaged than I had expected, from the long-endured pain I imagine, but the embarrassment a stranger might feel about this was tempered by the quizzical eyes and the warmth his presence gave off. (He kept on going to Augusta for the Masters until two years before the end. Mercifully, for everyone but his family, we would not see him when he could no longer bear to be seen).

After that first meeting I never again felt uncomfortable about his ailment, and only once did he mention it, which was when he spoke a sentence that has passed into the apocrypha. Pat well knew that Jones never talked about his disease but on that day he really wanted to penetrate the mask of courage and know just how good or bad things really were. Pat's expression was so candid that — I sensed — Jones felt he would, for once, say a word or two. He said that he'd been told that his disease occurred in two forms — "descending and ascending,[*] " that luckily his paralysis had been from the waist and his extremities down, so that, he added, "I have my heart and lungs and my so called brain." He spoke about it easily with a rueful smile, and no more was said. The familiar punch line, "You know, we play the ball where it lies," was not said in my presence and, I must say, it sounds to me false to Jones' character, as of a passing thought by a screenwriter that Hollywood would never resist. Let us thank God that Hollywood has never made a movie about Jones; it would almost surely be more inept and more molassic than the dreadful *Follow The Sun*, the alleged "epic" about Ben Hogan.

About the disease. At a tournament Jones was playing in in England, Henry

---

[*] I have consulted several neurologists about this. None is aware of this distinction but all say that it can begin by attacking different parts of the body in different victims.

Longhurst, the late, great rogue of English golf writing, was standing beside a doctor who, marveling at Jones' huge pivot, the long arch of his swing and the consequent muscular strain that sustained it, predicted that one day it would cause him grievous back trouble. Longhurst wrote and retailed this comment to Jones, who responded with a good-tempered note saying, with typical tact, that Henry was good to be concerned but the trouble was due to a rare disease. This sad turn in Jones' life has also received several versions. So far as I can discover, from tapping the memory of his oldest surviving friend, the inimitable Charlie Yates, and checking with the expertise of several medicos, the true account is simple and drastic.

In the summer of 1948, Jones remarked to Yates, in the middle of what was to be his last round ever, that he would not soon be playing again because his back had become unbearable and he was going to have to have an operation. It was, in fact, the first of two operations and it revealed damage to the spinal tissue that could not then be tagged with a definite diagnosis. A year or so later, Jones went up to Boston and after being examined at the Lahey Clinic had the second operation, during which a positive diagnosis was made: syringomyelia, a chronic progressive degenerative disease of the spinal cord, which, as we all know, Jones bore for 22 years with chilling stoicism. The scant consolation for the rest of us is that anyone falling victim to the same disease today could expect no better outcome. The etiology is still unknown and there is no cure.

When I first went into the sitting room of Jones' cottage at Augusta, I noticed at once a large picture over the mantelpiece, a framed series of cartoon strips by the best, and throughout the 1920's and '30s, the most famously popular English sports cartoonist, Tom Webster. No American I knew (and no Englishman under 70) had ever heard his name, but the drawings — of Jones and of Hagen, I believe — served as a tap root into Jones' memories of Britain and British golf in the Twenties. He enlightened me about the character and skill of various old heroes I brought up: Braid and Duncan and Tolley and Roger Wethered and, of course, Hagen. (Though I played no golf I followed it — from the papers, the newsreels, and the Webster cartoons — as zealously as I followed county cricket). This talk brought up, one time, the never-ending controversy about the essential characteristic of the good golf swing. Jones distrusted "keep your eye on the ball" almost as much as Tommy Armour did. His preference was for Abe Mitchell's "the player should move freely beneath himself."

Jones never recalled to me, as all famous athletes are apt to do, the acclaim of his great days, though once when I had just come back from St. Andrews, he remarked again what a "wonderful experience" it had been on his later visits "to go about a town where people wave at you from doorways and windows." Otherwise, he never said anything that made me doubt his friends' assurance that he was uncomfortable with the spotlight and was grateful to have room service in the hotels of towns where he would be recognized on the streets. He did not flaunt his trophies at home, and he kept his medals locked up in a chest.

Our talks were mostly about books, people, politics, only rarely about golf, whenever Ward-Thomas was eager for another Jones quote for his bulging file of golfing wisdom. In the winter after my first meeting, a book came out entitled *Bobby Jones On Golf*, and I reviewed it under the heading, "The Missing Aristotle Papers on Golf," remarking along the way that Jones' gift for distilling a complex emotion into the barest language would not have shamed John Donne; that his meticulous insistence on the right word to impress the right visual image was worthy of fussy old Flaubert; and that his unique personal gift was "to take apart many of the club clichés with a touch of grim Lippmannesque humor." Shortly after the piece appeared, Jones dropped me a letter beginning: "Off hand, I can't think of another contemporary author who has been compared in one piece to Aristotle, Flaubert, John Donne and Walter Lippman!"

> IN HIS INSTINCTS AND BEHAVIOR HE WAS WHAT USED TO BE CALLED A GENTLEMAN, AN IDEAL NOWADAYS MUCH DERIDED BY THE YOUNG AND THE LIBERATED.

Much was made — rightly — when the book came out about the extraordinary fact that Jones had written it himself. This is only to remark, in a more interesting way, how phenomenally rare it is for a scholar to become a world class athlete. The same dependence on a ghost is true of actors and actresses, as also of ninety percent of the world's — at least the Western world's — best politicians. The exceptions are rare indeed. Churchill, after a Washington wartime meeting with Roosevelt, flew home in a bomber, alternating between the controls and the composition of a speech on a pad. He was no sooner in London than he appeared at the B.B.C. and broadcast across the Atlantic a majestic strategical survey of the world at war. To his horror, Roosevelt heard it in the White House while he was working on his own promised broadcast with the aid of three ghost writers. One of them, Robert Sherwood, consoled the President with the sorrowful thought: "I'm afraid, Mr. President, he rolls his own."

When I think back to those Augusta talks, I recall most vividly the quality of irony that was always there in his eyes and often in his comments on people and things. I asked him once about "the master eye" without knowing that he had written about it. I'm sure he said what he had said before: he didn't believe in it or in the ritual of plumb bobbing. The main thing was to "locate the ball's position...I'm told a man can do this better with two eyes than with one." The last time I saw him, I told him about a rather morose Scottish caddie I'd recently had who took a dim view of most things American, but especially the golf courses, which — he'd been told — had lots of trees. We were sitting out on the porch of his Augusta cottage and Jones looked down at the towering pines, the great cathedral nave, of the plunging 10th fairway. "I don't see," he said deadpan, "any need for a tree on a golf course."

Toward the end of one Masters tournament, Henry Longhurst took suddenly very ill. He lay grumpily in his hospital bed and, lifting his ripe W.C. Fields' nose over the bedsheet, predicted that it was "closing time." Happily, it turned out not to be, but Pat and I stayed over through the Monday to watch out for him. In the early afternoon, when the place was empty, we called on Jones and he suggested we collect some clubs from the pro shop and play the splendid par three course. We were about to set off when Cliff Roberts, co-founder of the Club, came in. He was shocked at the generosity of Jones' suggestion: "Bob, you surely know the rule — no one can play without a member going along." "Don't you think," Jones asked wistfully, "you and I could exercise a little Papal indulgence?" Roberts did not think so. And although he'd recently had a major operation, he went off, got into his golfing togs and limped around with us through six holes, by which time he was ready for intensive care and staggered away accepting the horrid fact of the broken rule.

Because of the firm convention of writing nothing about Jones that is less than idolatrous, I have done a little digging among friends and old golfing acquaintances who knew him and among old writers who, in other fields, have a sharp nose for the disreputable. But I do believe that a whole team of investigative reporters, working in shifts like coal miners, would find that in all of Jones' life anyone had been able to observe, he nothing common did or mean.

The sum of what can be said about his character, by me at any rate, is: that he was an incurable conservative frequently shown in the company of tycoons (more their photo op, I suspect, than his) which led to his reputation for gregariousness ("they say I love people but I don't love people, I love a few people in small doses"); that he was a weekend golfer who rarely touched a club between October and March; that he showed a famous early streak of temper at St. Andrews when he was 19 for which he proffered "a general apology" on the spot and was ever afterward restrained. In his instincts and behavior he was what used to be called a gentleman, an ideal nowadays much derided by the young and the liberated.

For myself, I may be exposing my own inability to get much below the attractive surface of the man when I say that in my life I can count four human beings who radiated simple goodness: a Franciscan priest; a university professor; my father; and Robert Tyre Jones, Jr. Maybe "radiated" is too strong a word, for one striking thing about good human beings is their gift for not being striking. Jones had an instinct for noticing, and attending to, the shy one in any bubbling company. His capacity for shifting the spotlight away from himself was remarkable even in the one performance where you would expect him to be authoritative: in the act of teaching golf. In those precious film shorts he made for the Warner brothers, in which a lesson in the use of the brassie or mashie is tagged on to a ludicrous plot about a golf widow or other domestic strain, he never says "you must do this..." or "it is essential that you do that." He is careful always to say: "I've found that if I move the ball an inch or so..." and "perhaps if you tried...it works well with some people."

What we are left with in the end is a forever young, good-looking Southerner, an impeccably courteous and decent man with a private ironical view of life who, to the great good fortune of people who saw him, happened to play the great game with more magic and more grace than anyone before or since.

HIS STRENGTH OF MIND

BY DAVE ANDERSON

*I*n 1930, the year that Bobby Jones would forever gild with his Grand Slam, he had won the British Amateur at St. Andrews and the British Open at Hoylake. Now, on his way to Southampton for the return voyage on the *S.S. Europa* to the United States Open at Interlachen and the United States Amateur at Merion, he and his English rival, Cyril Tolley, were on a train rattling out of London into the countryside.

"Bob," asked Tolley, "how long have you been over here?"

"About six weeks," the 28-year-old Georgian replied.

"Do you suppose," Tolley asked, "you have ever played so badly for so long a period? And yet you have won both our championships."

Another golfer might have been offended, but Jones smiled.

"Cyril was trying to emphasize," he would write in his autobiography *Golf Is My Game*, "what I knew so well to be a fact: that I had managed by the hardest possible kind of labor to win these two tournaments when my game was never once anywhere near peak efficiency."

Of all the explanations for all of Bobby Jones' success, those few words of his might be the best. They were words shaped by advice from Long Jim Barnes, one of golf's forgotten legends: the winner of the 1916 and 1919 PGA championship, the 1921 U.S. Open and the 1925 British Open.

"Bob, you can't always be playing well," Barnes once told the golf prodigy who had played in his first U.S. Amateur at age 14. "You'll never win tournaments until you learn to score well when you're playing badly."

In winning four U.S. Opens, three British Opens, five U.S. Amateurs and one British Amateur in a span of seven years before he decided not to compete seriously any longer, Jones absorbed that lesson as few others have.

"I think this is what I learned to do best of all," he acknowledged in his elegant Southern accent. "The most acute, and yet the most satisfying recollections I have are of the tournaments won by triumphs over my own mistakes and by crucial strokes played with imagination and precision when anything ordinary would not have succeeded."

Until he died in 1971 at age 69 that same determination prolonged his triumph over syringomyelia, an incurable paralysis that demanded a cane, then leg braces and finally a wheelchair, but left his mind clear.

Bob Jones, age 14, in his first national competition, the 1916 U.S. Amateur Championship at Merion.

Bob Jones and Cyril Tolley, after the 1930 British Amateur and British Open, about to embark on the train taking them to the *SS Europa* bound for the United States.

"The man was sick and fought it for so long and fought it so successfully," Ben Hogan said after Jones' death, "I think we have finally discovered the secret of his success. It was the strength of his mind."

HE WAS AN AMATEUR GOLFER WHOSE TOWER OF TALENT INTIMIDATED THE TOURING PROS OF THAT ERA.

That strength of mind sculpted a Hollywood-handsome folk hero on a pedestal in the Roaring Twenties alongside those for Babe Ruth, Red Grange, Jack Dempsey and Bill Tilden. It developed the first great American golfer to whom only Jack Nicklaus and Hogan have been compared, the only celebrity to bask in two parades up lower Broadway in New York City.

He so dominated his era that from 1923 to 1930 his two primary rivals, Walter Hagen and Gene Sarazen, never won a United States Open or a British Open that he entered.

From age 20 to 28 he won the U.S. Open four times and was second four times; during that same age span Jack Nicklaus won the U.S. Open only twice and was second twice.

Bob Jones chats with Ben Hogan on his return from capturing the 1953 British Open at Carnoustie. Hogan had won the Masters and U.S. Open earlier that year, the closest anyone has come to a modern Grand Slam.

He was an amateur golfer whose tower of talent intimidated the touring pros of that era. Walter Hagen would bark at his fellow pros, "We've got to stop this kid." Tommy Armour, the 1927 U.S. Open champion, lost several friendly matches with Jones before finally accepting 1 up a side in their bets. Asked years later how he could do that with an amateur, Amour growled, "Because that's how goddam good he was."

He was more than a sweet swinger. Using hickory shafts and golf balls that stopped at least 30 yards shorter than today's balls would, he was the first golfer to reach the Olympic Club's 604-yard 16th hole in two.

He was truly, as Chi Chi Rodriguez once joked about Jack Nicklaus, "a legend in his spare time." He competed in only 52 tournaments but won 23, nearly half. "I don't play against men," he explained, "I play against par." No amateur ever beat him twice. He averaged only three months a year in traveling to and from tournaments. In his best years from 1923 to 1930 he played in only seven so-called ordinary tournaments, five of which were open events; he won four. He averaged only about 80 rounds a year at home.

After he stopped competing, he founded the Augusta National Golf Club and created The Masters Tournament along with his friend Clifford Roberts.

And as a person, Bobby Jones was more than a golfer. At 18, he was graduated in 1920 from Georgia Tech with a degree in mechanical engineering after only three

The leading figures in the 'Golden Age of Sport'.
Back row, left to right: Babe Ruth (baseball), Gene Tunney (boxing), Johnny Weismuller (swimming), Bill Cook (hockey).
Front row: Bill Tilden (tennis), Bob Jones (golf), Fred Spencer and Charley Winters (six-day bicycle racing).

years. At 21 he earned a degree in English from Harvard in 1923 after only three semesters. At 24, he entered Emory University Law School in Atlanta in 1926, but suddenly withdrew in his third semester to take the bar exam; he passed. For years he was a working day-to-day attorney.

During World War II, although deferred as a 40-year-old father of three (Clara, Robert Tyre III, and Mary Ellen) and also because of varicose veins, he was commissioned as an Army Air Force intelligence officer who served briefly in Europe under Gen. Dwight Eisenhower's command. He was discharged as a Lieut. Colonel.

Bob Jones during World War II.

As much as anything else, he was real. Without even trying, he upstaged W.C. Fields, Jimmy Cagney, Joe E. Brown and other Hollywood stars in his instructional films. He sang Puccini arias in a rich baritone and recited bawdy limericks. He could swear magnificently. He drank Prohibition corn whiskey. He didn't need his ego stroked. While at Harvard, he learned he was ineligible for the golf team because he was a Georgia Tech graduate. He asked to be the golf team's manager. Told there already was a manager, the runner-up in the 1922 U.S. Open asked to be the assistant manager.

"How else," he explained, "am I going to get a crimson 'H' letter?"

For the Harvard-Yale match at the Rhode Island Country Club that year, the assistant manager had one responsibility: safely transport the whiskey for the anticipated celebration. While riding to the match with the manager in the rumble seat of a roadster on a chilly day, the whiskey somehow disappeared.

"Between the two of them," a member of that Harvard team once said, "they drank every ounce of it."

Many years later, asked to write his autobiography, he wrote it himself, as he had dozens of magazine articles and newspaper columns. He wrote as graciously as he lived. In an article in *The American Golfer* magazine, he modestly described a friendly round at St. Andrews with Joyce Wethered after the first of his Grand Slam triumphs.

"She did not miss one shot," he wrote of the legendary British amateur whose brother, Roger, he had defeated in that year's British Amateur final. "She did not even half-miss one shot. I could not help saying that I had never played golf with anyone, man or woman, amateur or professional, who made me feel so utterly outclassed."

Through it all he quietly accepted being known or addressed by the diminutive Bobby, although he preferred Bob.

"Listen to this letter from a third-grader," he once told a friend in his understanding manner. "Dear Bobby: When I grow up I want to be an engineer. What do you want to be when you grow up?"

Maybe he remembered when he was a third-grader, when he was already considered to be a golf Phenom.

Joyce Wethered.

Named for his paternal grandfather, Robert Tyre Jones, Jr. was born on March 17, 1902, in Atlanta, Ga., but he was a sickly child. When he was five his father, an attor-

Bob Jones at six years of age.

USGA

ney, moved the family for the summer to a boarding house near the East Lake Country Club, then at the end of the trolley line. His first club was a neighbor's gift, a cutdown cleek, a version of what is now a 1-iron. While playing with his sister Clara and their friend Frank Meador, he hit scuffed golf balls with that cleek on a two-hole course; one hole was near the house, the other near a deep drainage ditch.

"It is the general opinion that I never made a hole-in-one until 1927," he once said with a smile. "As a matter of fact, I made that ditch hole many times in one before I was six years old."

The next year, with his family now living in what had been the mule house on the East Lake property, six-year-old Bobby fetched water from the nearest well when he wasn't playing golf. In his first competitive tournament against two other boys and Alexa Stirling, later a three-time U.S. Women's Amateur champion, he won the six-hole event.

"I'm prouder," he would say years later, "of that little silver cup than any other trophy."

The first trophy.

JULES ALEXANDER / ATLANTA HISTORY CENTER

His talent was honed by imitation. Instead of taking formal lessons, he learned how to swing a golf club by tagging along behind Stewart Maiden, the East Lake pro, whenever the wee Scotsman was playing 18 holes with the members.

USGA

Bob Jones, Perry Adair and Frank Meador.

"Stewart's method was simple," he recalled. "He merely stepped up to the ball and hit it, which to the end of my playing days was always a characteristic of my play."

His play matured quickly. At nine he won the Atlanta Athletic Club junior title against a 16-year-old opponent. At 13 he won an invitational in Birmingham, Ala.; at 14 he won the East Lake Invitational and the Georgia Amateur, defeating his friend Perry Adair in the 36-hole final. Adair's father had already planned to shepherd his son to the 1916 U.S. Amateur at Merion, but now, with the Jones family's permission, he took 14-year-old Bobby too. Pudgy at 5' 4", wearing his first pair of long pants and with golf spikes screwed into brown Army shoes, the Jones boy stunned Eben Byers, the 1906 champion, and Frank Dyer, the Pennsylvania Amateur champion, before losing in the third round, 5 and 3, to Bob Gardner, the defending champion. Had Jones won that Amateur, he would have reigned until 1919 because World War I canceled the 1917 and 1918 tournaments, but in retrospect he considered that loss a blessing.

"I shudder to think what those years might have done to me," he would acknowledge later, alluding to the burden of a three-year reign as a national champion as a teenager. "Not so much to my golf, but in a vastly more important respect, to me as a human being."

No golfer, not even Nicklaus, has ever been so precocious on a national level. But he needed time to grow in skill and self-control. One of his favorite stories involved his pairing as an 18-year-old with 50-year-old Harry Vardon while qualify-

The J. Carroll Payne Tournament trophy won by Bob Jones in 1913.

JULES ALEXANDER / ATLANTA ATHLETIC CLUB

ing for the 1920 U.S. Open at Inverness. The teenager and the venerable English pro hadn't spoken to each other until Jones took a bogey on the seventh hole after skulling a pitch shot over the green into heavy rough. On their way to the eighth tee, he turned to the six-time British Open champion.

"I said, 'Mr. Vardon, have you ever seen a worse shot?'" he often recalled with a laugh. "All he said was, 'No.'"

But there would be a worse moment for this sometimes hotheaded teenager. In his first British Open in 1921 at St. Andrews, he played so poorly in the third round that he tore up his scorecard.

"It was," he would reflect later, "the most inglorious failure of my golfing life."

In retrospect, it was also the most significant turning point of his golfing life. He would acknowledge that tearing up his scorecard was a "childish effort to make known publicly that such a misplay was not to be tolerated by a player of so much ability." Two years later he might have withered after another misplay. Just off the 18th green in two on the final hole of the 1923 U.S. Open at Inwood, he flubbed his chip shot and needed three more strokes for a 76, allowing Bobby Cruickshank to force an 18-hole playoff.

The next day, all even going to the 18th, a long par 4 with water guarding the green. Cruickshank hit a bad drive, forcing him to lay up in front of the pond. Jones' long drive had bounced through the right rough onto hard ground about 200 yards away. Jones now had a decision: lay up and probably need another 18-hole playoff, or go for the green and a victory but risk a splash that might mean a loss. He chose to go for it. His 2-iron off the dirt rose like an arrow, landed 10 feet short of the hole and stopped seven feet beyond it.

With a 76 Bobby Jones was the U.S. Open champion, his first national title. At 21, he had begun what his Boswell and friend, O.B. Keeler, would describe as the "Seven Fat Years" that followed what *The Atlanta Journal* sportswriter called the "Seven Lean Years."

But not even Jones won every tournament, or even won a tournament every year. Two months later in the U.S. Amateur at Flossmoor outside Chicago he lost, 2 and 1, in the quarterfinals to Max Marston, the eventual champion. He would win the Amateur in both 1924 and 1925, but he lost the 1925 U.S. Open to Willie Macfarlane in a 36-hole playoff at the Worcester (Mass.) Country Club after having called a one-stroke penalty on himself over the protests of rules officials.

During the first round Jones noticed his ball move slightly in the rough as his iron grazed the grass. When he informed the officials, they told him they hadn't seen the ball move. Neither

The 1911 Junior Golf Championship trophy of the Atlanta Athletic Club.

Robert Gardner, Chick Evans, Perry Adair and Bob Jones in the Red Cross Matches played during World War I.

Bob Jones and Harry Vardon at the 1920 U.S. Open at Inverness.

had anyone in the gallery. But he insisted. Although it's difficult to assume that every stroke thereafter would have been the same, that penalty stroke would be the difference between Jones' winning and the playoff he lost. But he refused to accept praise for observing the rule.

"You might as well praise a man," he said "for not robbing a bank."

Those words were now the mark of the man, as well as the mark of what golf is supposed to be. In what was considered then to be the gentleman's game, the tempestuous teenager was now golf's glorious gentleman.

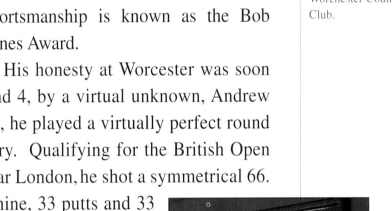

Willie Macfarlene defeated Bob Jones by one stroke in a 36-hole playoff for the 1925 U.S. Open at the Worchester Country Club.

...THE TEMPESTUOUS TEENAGER WAS NOW GOLF'S GLORIOUS GENTLEMAN.

Significantly, the United States Golf Association's award for distinguished sportsmanship is known as the Bob Jones Award.

His honesty at Worcester was soon rewarded. In 1926, after being stunned, 5 and 4, by a virtual unknown, Andrew Jamieson, in the British Amateur at Muirfield, he played a virtually perfect round that still stands like a monument to his artistry. Qualifying for the British Open over Sunningdale's 6,472-yard Old Course near London, he shot a symmetrical 66. He had 33 on the front nine, 33 on the back nine, 33 putts and 33 other strokes. He missed only one green in regulation, but saved par. He had six birdies and no bogeys.

The plaque for the Bob Jones Award hangs in the museum at Golf House, the USGA's headquarters in New Jersey.

"After a reverential cheer at the final green," Bernard Darwin wrote in *The Times* of London, "the crowd dispersed awestruck, realizing they had witnessed something they had never seen before and would never see again."

Jones would call it "the best round of golf I ever played in competition." O.B. Keeler, who covered all 31 of the national championships that Jones entered, would write, "There have been lower scoring rounds; Bobby himself has scored better. But this card of 66 was played with a precision and freedom from error never attained before or after. It was incomparable in steadiness of execution."

The day before Jones had acquired a driver from the Sunningdale pro. Nicknamed "Jeannie Deans" after the heroine of Sir Walter Scott's novel, "The Heart of Midlothian," that driver would help him win 10 titles in his final 13 national championships. So would his new putter, Calamity Jane II.

Jones had begun putting with his original Calamity Jane after a friendly round at the Nassau Country Club on Long Island before the 1923 U.S. Open at Inwood. On the 18th green Jim Maiden, the older brother of the East Lake pro, heard Jones complaining about his putting and handed him a thin-bladed putter he had named for the old West's woman sharpshooter. With his first stroke, Jones holed a 30-footer.

Bob Jones was defeated in the sixth round of the 1926 British Amateur at Muirfield by Andrew Jamison.

"I'd like to keep this club," he said.

"Put it in your bag," Jim Maiden said.

Jones won the U.S. Open at Inwood, his first major, but he eventually realized that the old putter's smooth but uneven face created mis-hits. He had J. Victor East at Spalding make six copies. He gave five to friends and kept the one he used at Sunningdale during his 66 and would use thereafter. With his new Calamity Jane II and now his new Jeannie

Calamity Jane II hangs proudly in Golf House.

JULES ALEXANDER / USGA

Deans driver, he won the British Open at Royal Lytham and St. Annes a week later, prompting his first ticker-tape parade up Broadway on his return.

When he won the 1926 U.S. Open at Scioto a few weeks later he was the first to win the two Open titles in the same year. In his Columbus, Ohio, hotel room that night, he collapsed in tears from the public's expectations that now were his burden. He almost won that year's U.S. Amateur too, losing in the final to George Von Elm, 2 and 1.

In 1927 he won the British Open again, slipped to a tie for 11th in the U.S. Open (his worst finish except for having missed the cut in 1920) and won the U.S. Amateur. In 1928 he lost another U.S. Open 36-hole playoff, by one stroke to Johnny Farrell at Olympia Fields outside Chicago, but won his fourth U.S. Amateur at Brae Burn outside Boston, routing Thomas Perkins of England in the final, 10 and 9.

In 1929 he won his third U.S. Open, by 23 strokes in a 36-hole playoff with Al Espinosa at Winged Foot after holing an excruciating clutch putt: a 12-foot downhill left-to-right slider on the final green that he had needed to create a tie.

On the 25th anniversary of that memorable putt, Winged Foot cut a ceremonial hole approximately where the cup had been that day in 1929 and four U.S. Open champions tried to make the putt: Gene Sarazen, Tommy Armour, Johnny Farrell and Craig Wood. None did. Then again, none were as desperate as Jones had been after suffering through two 7's in his final round. And few would have been as thoughtful as Jones was minutes later. Knowing he was in a Sunday playoff with Espinosa, he turned to Herbert Ramsay, the USGA vice-president.

"What time tomorrow?" he asked.

"Nine and one," Ramsay replied.

"Let's start in the morning at 10," Jones said. "Al will want to go to Mass."

"Ten and two," Ramsay agreed.

Jones, whose wife Mary was a Catholic, accompanied her to Mass the next morning, then he blistered Espinosa, 72-69—141 to 84-80—164, for his third U.S. Open title. But at the U.S. Amateur at Pebble Beach, he was upset in the first round by Johnny Goodman, 1 up. Suddenly and shockingly, he had been stung in the tournament he considered the easiest for him to win, and in the first round. But he realized the mistake of his anxiety in 18-hole matches, which he considered too short for form always to prevail, in contrast to his confidence over 36 holes.

ASSOCIATED PRESS

George Von Elm defeated Jones in the finals of the 1926 U.S. Amateur.

Johnny Farrell defeated Bob by one stroke in a 36-hole playoff for the 1928 U.S. Open.

BILLY FARRELL

"I really lost," he would explain, "because I was in too big a hurry to overcome Goodman's lead and to seize command. But from that day on, I was able to play all matches in the same way."

Jones also realized that in 1930 the Walker Cup team's trip to Britain would allow him to play all four major tournaments in the same year; in 1926 he had won both Opens and gone to the U.S. Amateur final.

"I have been frequently confronted," he would write, "with the question, 'Had I started out the year 1930 with the expectation, or even hope, of winning the four major championships?' I did not feel like saying that I had, because I felt reluctant to admit that I considered myself capable of such an accomplishment. Actually, I did make my plans for that golfing year with precisely this end in view."

Instead of adding a few pounds during the Winter months, Jones often played a form of badminton. Instead of waiting until April to begin serious golf, he played in two Georgia tournaments against touring pros, losing in Savannah to Horton Smith by one stroke and winning the Southeastern Open at Augusta by 13 strokes.

Soon he was off to Royal St. George's where he captained the winning Walker Cup team, then to St. Andrews for the British Amateur, a tournament he had never won. If he didn't survive seven 18-hole matches and a 36-hole final, his Grand Slam quest would be empty. He survived, twice barely. He needed 19 holes to get by Cyril Tolley, the husky Englishman who was a two-time champion, after holing an eight-foot par putt at the 17th, the famous Road Hole, to stay even. In the semifinals he was 2 down with five to play against George Voigt, his Walker Cup teammate, but rallied to win with a par on the 18th after holing a 12-foot par putt on the 17th to stay even. In the 36-hole final he dominated Roger Wethered, 7 and 6.

When he won the British Open at Hoylake by two strokes over Leo Diegel and Macdonald Smith despite a double-bogey 7 at the eighth hole in the final round, he was halfway to what George Trevor of *The New York Sun* would call The Impregnable Quadrilateral.

Not long after his second ticker-tape parade up Broadway, he arrived in Minneapolis for the U.S. Open at Interlachen. He opened with a 71, two under par but one off the lead shared by Tommy Armour and Macdonald Smith, on what he would call "the hottest day I can ever remember." His red tie was so knotted, O.B. Keeler had to cut it off with a pocket knife. One leg of his sweat-soaked light-gray plus fours was stained red from the tees in his pocket. His second-round 73 dropped him two behind Horton Smith, but provided his legendary "lily pad" shot: a half-topped spoon that skidded across a pond onto the bank in front of the

RALPH W. MILLER LIBRARY

LOS ANGELES PUBLIC LIBRARY

Top: Bob Jones congratulates Johnny Goodman on the 18th hole at Pebble Beach after Goodman defeated him one down in the 1929 U.S. Amateur. This was the first and only time Bob had lost in the first round of the U.S. Amateur.

Above: Bob Jones with Roger Lapham, President of the California Golf Association, and Prescott Bush, the Secretary of the USGA at the 1929 Amateur.

THE BETTMANN ARCHIVE

Bob Jones with his family in 1933: Bob III, Clara and wife Mary holding Mary Ellen.

ninth green. After pitching to within four feet, he holed his birdie putt.

"Actually, no lily pad was involved," he often explained. "The action of the ball was precisely that of a flat stone being skipped across the water."

Despite bogies on the last two holes in Saturday morning's third round, his 68 opened a five-stroke lead. Despite three double-bogey 5's in the afternoon, his 40-foot putt on the 18th produced a final-round 75 in the afternoon for 287, two strokes better than Macdonald Smith and five ahead of Horton Smith. For the fourth time, he had won the U.S. Open against all the best pros.

> ## "THE MOST TRIUMPHANT JOURNEY ANY MAN EVER TRAVELED IN SPORT."

To complete the Grand Slam all he had to do now was defeat five amateurs at Merion for his fifth U.S. Amateur title. But lightning and a runaway car nearly deprived him of his opportunity.

Jones was putting on the 12th green at East Lake during a casual round when a lightning bolt slammed into the 10th fairway only 40 yards away. As he ran for the clubhouse, another bolt slashed a tree near the 13th tee. Just as he arrived safely at the clubhouse, another bolt shattered the chimney above the locker-room entrance. Not long after that, as he walked to the Downtown Atlanta A.C. for lunch, he suddenly heard a voice behind him yell, "Look out, mister." Turning, he jumped away from a driverless car that crashed into the wall of the Atlanta A.C. clubhouse. It had silently rolled down a hill and hopped the sidewalk.

After those two close calls, the U.S. Amateur was a lark. No longer uneasy in 18-hole matches, he quickly dominated Sandy Somerville, the Canadian Amateur champion, and Fred Hoblitzel, another Canadian, each by 5 and 4. In the scheduled 36-hole matches of the ensuing rounds, he disposed of Fay Coleman, a Californian, 3 and 2, then routed Jess Sweetser, the 1922 U.S. Amateur champion, 9 and 8, in the semifinals. In the final he crushed Gene Homans, out of Englewood (N.J.), 8 and 7. After holing the winning putt on the 11th green, four dozen Marines in dress-blues escorted him through the record gallery of 18,000 to Merion's white clubhouse.

"The most triumphant journey," William D. Richardson would write in *The New York Times*, "any man ever traveled in sport."

After the trophy presentation, Jones disappeared into the Merion clubhouse for a drink with O.B. Keeler and Grantland Rice.

"All the time, I'm standing in the corner with his bag of clubs," his caddie, Howard Rexford, would recall. "He had 18 clubs; there wasn't a 14-club limit like there is now. He had six woods, as I remember. After a while he came out, thanked me and put some money in my hand. I didn't even look at it. He took his clubs. I went outside and hid and looked. There were 15 ten-dollar bills, $150. In the

Bob Jones shows Jimmy Johnson the results of 1930 in the front parlor of his home. Having won all four major titles, as well as being the captain of the victorious Walker Cup team, the Walker Cup was sent to Jones to display with the other trophies.

John Kelly, Bob's caddy, with Jones' golf clubs in 1928.

Depression, that was a real fortune."

Seven weeks later, in an unsentimental letter to the USGA, a 28-year-old Bobby Jones announced his retirement from championship golf.

> ... HE NEVER STOPPED BEING FRIENDLY, BEING GRACIOUS, BEING HIMSELF.

In the years that followed he was always busy. He concentrated on his law practice. He signed a $101,000 contract with Warner Brothers for 12 instructional short subjects with an option, soon picked up, for six more at an additional fee; all are now on videotape. He designed Spalding's first matched set of flanged irons. He founded and built Augusta National, then created the Masters.

"Our overall aim at the Augusta National," he wrote, "has been to provide a golf course of considerable natural beauty, relatively easy for the average golfer to play, and at the same time testing for the expert player striving to better par figures."

In a ceremonial appearance at the first Masters in 1934, he shot 76-74-72-72—294, tying for 13th place. He would tee off in ten more Masters, but never finish that high again.

Bob and Mary Jones at the premier for the movie *Gone With The Wind* in Atlanta.

Three generations of Joneses: Bob, his grandson and his son.

But mostly Jones played golf at East Lake with old friends or sometimes with members he hardly knew. He had a reputation, as Gene Sarazen said, of making "you feel that you were playing with a friend, and you were." In one of those friendly rounds at East Lake in 1948, he was two under par after 16 holes when he suddenly pulled his drive into the rough.

"We had started on the 10th, so we were at the 8th," his friend Tommy Barnes said. "I had never seen Bob hit a bad drive in my life. He made a double-bogey there and finished even par."

Jones would never play another 18-hole round. Bothered in previous weeks by back and neck pain, he had been losing strength in his right arm and right leg. Tests showed bone growths on three cervical vertebrae. Surgery didn't help. Over the next two years the pain spread to his left side. More surgery didn't ease the pain. Not until 1956 was the diagnosis complete: syringomyelia, a rare and degenerative disease of the central nervous system.

His life became agony now, his every movement tortured by his illness. He would need braces on his legs, then crutches and eventually a wheelchair. But he never stopped being friendly, being gracious, being himself.

"Just think," he said, "I'll never again have to worry about a three-foot putt."

Even in a wheelchair, he continued to work at his law office. He would stop by East Lake for a drink. He smoked two packs of

Old friends Bob Jones and Gene Sarazen at the filming of Shell's "Wonderful World of Golf" at Peachtree Golf Club in the late 1960's.

cigarettes a day, slipping each one into a special holder and saying, "I've got to give these things up." During the Masters he would stay in his white cottage near the 10th tee and watch the tournament evolve on television. One year one of his long-time friends among the British golf writers, Pat Ward-Thomas, stopped by to ask about his health.

"Well, Pat," he replied, "I have my heart, my lungs and my so-called brain. We play it as it lies."

About a week after converting to Catholicism to please his wife Mary, he died in his sleep on December 18, 1971, of an aneurysm. He was buried in Oakland cemetery in Atlanta below a tombstone of white Georgian marble chiseled with the only words he requested:

Robert Tyre Jones, Jr.

Born 1902   Died 1971

During his final years at the Masters, he had been wheeled out of his cottage to preside at the green-jacket ceremony. In 1965 a husky blond golfer named Jack Nicklaus won by nine strokes with a record 72-hole total of 271 and Jones' tribute to him has endured almost as much as his Grand Slam.

"Jack is playing an entirely different game," he said, "a game I'm not even familiar with."

But in his time, Bobby Jones played a game with that everybody else was not even familiar with. Being the best of his time is all that you can ask of any golfer, whether it was Ben Hogan or Jack Nicklaus, who has often acknowledged that Bobby Jones had been his inspiration. Nicklaus would win 20 major championships (six Masters, four U.S. Opens, three British Opens, five PGA's, two U.S. Amateurs).

At the Metropolitan Golf Writers Association Dinner in New York, Bob Jones greets Maureen Orcutt as 1960 U.S. Amateur Champion Jack Nicklaus and Vice President Richard Nixon look on. The globe-shaped trophy emblassoned with two American and two British flags, identifying the locations of the tournamants, was presented to Jones by the Vice President on the 30th anniversary of the Grand Slam.

But how many more majors would Jones have won had he competed beyond the age of 28? How many PGA's would he have won if he had been a pro?

At the 1976 U.S. Open at the Atlanta Athletic Club, a site chosen by the USGA at Jones' request, Jack Nicklaus was asked which of the great golfers he would most like to oppose in a Great Challenge Match in the Sky.

"Jones," he said.

At what course?

"St. Andrews. We both won the British Open there, and it's the home of golf."

Medal or match?

"It wouldn't make much difference."

Who would win?

"I would hope that he would think he would win, and I would hope that I would think that I would win."

You might say that this Great Challenge Match would be decided by what could be called strength of mind.

IN A CLASS BY HIMSELF

BY BEN CRENSHAW

Robert Tyre Jones, Jr. will forever be in a class by himself to my way of thinking. And I am not alone, by any means. For from this man we learn not only how we may improve our golf games and act like gentlemen, but also how to cope with life, however good or bad it may be. As Herbert Warren Wind has said, "As a young man he was able to stand up to just about the best that life can offer, and later he stood up with equal grace to just about the worst." Millions of words have been written about Bob Jones, but this quote sums it up. We can never quite describe the man he was; we can only try to learn from his example what golf and life are all about.

Bob Jones at 13 months of age.

Bob Jones was born a sick child, and was not expected to live more than a few years. The boy seemed to be allergic to every food given him, but he gradually outgrew this phase, and at an early age began playing sports, namely golf and baseball. He lived near the grounds of the East Lake course of the Atlanta Athletic Club, and golf had, it seemed, a singular fascination to him. He was fortunate in many respects to play golf in early childhood, and he was fortunate to meet East Lake's Scottish professional, Stewart Maiden, a teacher who had the common sense not to disrupt his rare natural talent.

Jones would simply watch Maiden and mimic him. I believe this is the way in which young golfers, at least the natural ones, are made. Jones never had a formal lesson from his teacher; only a few words and a few balls would restore his timing and he was on his way.

An oil painting of the East Lake Golf Club.

Bob Jones on the Chevy Chase course in 1921.

Before the 1925 U. S. Open, held at the Worcester Country Club, Jones was playing so badly that he telephoned Maiden, begging him to come up from Atlanta on the night train to help him. The next day, they went to the practice tee. After Jones had hit a few balls, Maiden said, "Why don't you try hitting it on your backswing?! Then he turned and left to go back to the clubhouse. The lesson was over.

Indeed, Jones was taking the club back far too quickly. Once he slowed his takeaway, he went on to tie for first. He was still tied after the first 18-hole playoff against Willie Macfarlane, and only lost by a single stroke in the second 18-hole playoff.

*I*ncidentally, Maiden also taught Alexa Stirling, Jones' childhood friend. Stirling won the Women's Amateur three times in a row—in 1916, 1919 and 1920—and was also three times runner-up. Like Jones, she imitated the Scotsman's Carnoustie swing, and owned the same rounded, and smooth action. Incredibly, artwork and photos of the two show the same identical finish to the full swing—with the club across the back of the neck.

The young Jones' skill at golf grew to awesome proportions when he was still in his teens, so much that the public placed upon him incredible pressure—pressure that would dog him until after he retired from competitive golf at the age of 28. Twenty-eight! That is almost laughable today, when most golfers are just coming into their prime in their twenties. The only champion golfer who retired almost as quickly was the fabulous

The master teacher and his students: Alexa Stirling, Bob Jones, Stewart Maiden and Perry Adair.

> IT MUST HAVE RILED THE YOUNG JONES TO BE PICKED BY EVERYONE TO WIN FOR SEVEN YEARS AND COME SO CLOSE SO OFTEN—AND THEN FAIL TO WIN.

Byron Nelson, at age 34, after he had collected enough trophies to stretch from Amarillo to Brownsville.

One of the reasons for Jones' early retirement was the fact that he was inwardly high strung. So much that he regularly would lose 10 to 15 pounds during a championship. So much that his only form of relaxation would be to ingest two stiff drinks and soak in a hot tub of water. When a championship was over, he would burst into tears without provocation. Jones had a hell of a temper during his early years, regularly tossing clubs about, and once tore up his scorecard during his first British Open in 1921 at the course he would come to admire the most—the Old Course at St. Andrews. Somehow

he learned to control his temper, and began winning the championships everyone expected him to win for such a long time, starting with the 1923 U.S. Open at Inwood on Long Island.

O.B. Keeler, the *Atlanta Journal* journalist who would accompany Jones on most of his travels, described Jones' golf years in halves, "the Seven Lean Years and the Seven Fat Years." How truly lean and fat they were.

It must have riled the young Jones to be picked by everyone to win for seven years and come so close so often—and then fail to win. This was the first test of his character.

Once he had won that first U. S. Open, he virtually exploded, winning 13 major golf tournaments by the time he was 28. He saved the best for last, ending his career brilliantly with the Grand Slam, winning the national opens and amateurs of the United States and Great Britain in one year. Despite all these triumphs and the adulation it brought him,

An oil painting of Alexa Stirling. Note the similarity to the finish of the Maiden taught "Carnoustie" swing of Bob Jones'.

he somehow managed to remain humble and unaffected. This was the second test of character. That Jones was genuine through all these tribulations and triumphs was only one reason he was loved so by the public on both sides of the Atlantic. The third test of Bob Jones' character would come later.

While he was piling up an unprecedented string of championships, the public began to embrace his literary side as well. When Jones put his thoughts on paper, the results were as elegant as his swing. To think that he wrote *Down the Fairway* at

Grantland Rice, one of America's finest-ever sports writers, greets Bob Jones after a round.

the age of 25 boggles the mind. And at the time, he had already earned a Mechanical Engineering degree at Georgia Tech and an English Literature degree at Harvard. Jones enrolled in Emory University Law School in Atlanta and passed the Bar Examination after two years. He then began to practice law with his father's firm. Later, he wrote two more books, *Golf is My Game* and *Bobby Jones on Golf*, and was a regular contributor to Grantland Rice's wonderful publication, *The American Golfer.*

Jones expressed himself in a way that was very human, baring his soul to us. Who else could say about golf championships and pressure, "One always feels that one is running from something without knowing what or where it is"? About golf in general he wrote, "Golf is the one game I know which becomes more and more difficult the longer one plays it."

Bob Jones was one of the very finest putters ever to play the game.

On putting and the often-used cliché "never up, never in," Jones said, "of course we never know but that the ball which is on line and stops short would have holed out. But we do know the ball that ran past did not hole out."

I might add that this system of "the dying putt" has always been the basis of my own view of putting. It seems to me that the object of putting is to leave the ball around the hole in order to make the next stroke simpler in proportion. The ball which arrives at the hole with the proper speed has an infinitely greater chance of *falling* in the hole from *any* entrance. Harvey Penick taught me the value of this method at an early age. This is what he meant by "giving luck a chance."

Jones was the most beloved golfer of his time, by his colleagues as well as his fans. He treated everyone with respect and courtesy and he was a true sportsman. He instinctively shifted the spotlight away from himself. He cherished his privacy and always felt quite nervous in front of a large gallery. In essence, he simply played a game he was enchanted with. Once a sports writer told Jones that he appeared unpretentious; at once he exclaimed "Pretension? What the hell is there to be pretentious about?" His acceptance speeches were short and to the point, and one came away with the impression that he thought it would be in poor taste to tread on anyone's time. In the same way, he thought golf should be

Admiring crowds were a fixture when Jones played.

played as quickly as possible. He simply walked up to the ball and hit it with that artful, powerful swing of his and then let matters take their course. Playing quickly was only natural to him, for in doing so he would not be a burden on his opponents.

After his Grand Slam year in 1930, Jones began to look for opportunities

The portrait taken by Hollywood photographer Elmer Fryer at the time Bob made the instructional films for Warner Brothers.

which might become meaningful and lasting. He signed a contract with Warner Brothers to do an instructional series called *"How I Play Golf."* This series of 18 skits, in which the major motion picture stars of the day were interwoven with small lessons fit beautifully with Jones's aim. They are a work of art to this day.

> ## BOBBY JONES' WRITINGS ON GOLF WERE A GIFT OF IMMENCE PROPORTIONS TO THE GAME.

Harvey Penick dedicated his life to helping others play their best golf. We talked often of how Stewart Maiden would offer just a few simple words of advice that would restore confidence quickly in the young and talented Jones. The point, at least to Harvey and me, was that, if an intelligent being with so much genius for golf could be "righted" so quickly, why would any teacher confuse their pupil with unnecessary information. Harvey, like Maiden, knew what and how to say to a pupil and no more. Just as a Scot — might, happily, I would add.

Bobby Jones' writings on golf were a gift of immense proportions to the game. They had a wide appeal, for he would say something, which, in my mind would be of similar value to the average golfer as well. Harvey thought they contained so much common sense, and he thought anyone could benefit from Jones' thoughts. To me, his style of writting was as elegant as his own swing, and his philosophies and viewpoints, as well as his command of the English language, will always be an important part of golf's literature.

Next would come the search for property to build Jones' ideal golf course, an idea that was brought to the attention of the public in a wry way. After Jones had won his third championship of the year in 1930, the U.S. Open at Interlachen, he was asked by a sports writer what he would do upon retiring. Jones turned to Keeler, his close companion, and said, "You'd better tell them now, O.B. You know." Keeler began quoting Hilaire Belloc's lines:

"If I ever become a rich man, / Or if ever I grow to be old, / I will build a house with deep thatch / To shelter me from the cold.../ I will hold my house in the high wood / Within a walk of the sea, / And the men that were boys when I was a boy / Shall sit and drink with me."

Jones' thoughts on his "dream course" had already started to take shape. To collaborate with him, he had chosen Dr. Alister Mackenzie, the famous Scottish architect, who was a fellow lover of St. Andrews. After searching for some time, the ideal property was found in Augusta. Jones

Dr. Alistair Mackenzie.

often traveled there for business and pleasure, as his wife Mary was from this beautiful town also. The property was called Fruitlands, a commercial nursery owned by a Belgian family named Berckmans. The land was just rare enough for Jones' and Mackenzie's taste, and work started on the course as soon as the land was purchased. Together they would build Augusta National, a course that would forever change American golf course architecture, a combination allowing the average player enough freedom from worry, but at the same time a course that exacts a thrilling test for the expert.

Mary Jones in 1949.

Augusta National Golf Club, the Masters and Bob Jones have been a major part of my life. I have enjoyed learning about each over the years, and they appeal to my own senses as well. I have been fortunate to have played some of the best golf of my career there. Having won the Masters twice now, my favorite tournament, at Bob Jones' Club, the same week we buried Harvey Penick, well ... one might imagine what these things mean to me.

The clubhouse at the Augusta National Golf Club at Masters time.

The third test of Jones' character was one of the cruelest things one could imagine. A serious problem with a stiff and sore neck and shoulder muscles began to develop even as early as his playing days. This condition gradually worsened and in 1948 Robert Tyre Jones, Jr. played his last game of golf. He had worn a brace on his right leg and had also undergone several unsuccessful operations to relieve pain and to remove bone growth on his spine. At New York's Columbia-Presbyterian Medical Center, he was diagnosed as having syringomyelia, a disease as rare as Jones himself. With his condition steadily deteriorating, Jones had to summon all the courage and dignity he had to fight it and accept it. He simply made up his mind that he would do the best that he could.

A small cup presented by the USGA in commemoration of the 25th anniversary of the Grand Slam.

In the late sixties he continued to travel to Augusta to attend the Masters and the presentation ceremony, but now he was permanently in a wheelchair, a helpless cripple. He still loved the company of his friends, and they would come by his cabin near the tenth tee to say hello and visit or report to him what scores were being shot. One of these close friends was Charles Price, the golf writer who helped edit *Bobby Jones on Golf*. One day while they were alone, Charlie could not conceal his emotions. Seeing his friend in this helpless state, he allowed a tear to slip down his cheek. Jones, I am sure, appreciated Price's deep feelings toward him, but he said softly, "Now Charles, we will have none of that; we all must play the ball as it lies."

A gold medal honoring Bob Jones' service as a USGA Committeeman from 1937 to 1971.

I never hope to hear of a stronger inner will or a truer determination to accept one's fate. Bob Jones was indeed in a class by himself.

"My, But You're A Wonder, Sir!"

BY PETER DOBEREINER

*H*e signed himself 'Bob'. His wife, Mary, called him Bob. He was Bob to his family. His friends addressed him as Bob. So why is he universally remembered today as Bobby Jones? The responsibility must be laid squarely at the door of the Scots. They have this habit of adding the affectionate-diminutive suffix of 'y' or 'ie' to any person or object which catches their fancy, often in association with the adjective 'wee', as in 'wee lassie.' Thus, Robert Burns became Rabbie when he became a literary lion and he in turn lapsed into the national whimsy in his ode to a mouse, which begins: "Wee sleekit, cow'rin', tim'rous beastie.' At least, when the Scots hijacked Mr. R. T. Jones Jun and set him up as a Caledonian icon they spared him the indignity of calling him Wee Bobby.

Hijacked? That is a slightly strong term, you may feel. Not really. We are all children of our history and for hundreds of years Scotland was subjected to rapine and pillage by marauding Norsemen from across the North Sea. The Scots gave as good as they got in the business of hijacking and they in turn made raids across the English border and appropriated all the cattle they could find. The English took a horrible revenge. A knight returning from the defence of Christianity in the Crusades against the hordes of Islam, brought back a souvenir in the form of a Persian musical instrument and allowed the Scots to adopt this bagpipe as their own. Then a Manchester wool merchant, dissatisfied with the meagre amount of cloth he could sell for the making of pants, invented a garment requiring twenty yards of tweed and conned the Scots into appropriating the kilt as their national dress.

The most barefaced act of Scottish larceny was to take the long established Dutch game of golf and brazenly stamp it: 'Made in Scotland.' To be fair, they nourished and formalised and improved golf to the extent that they truly made it into their national game. But by the Twenties the supply of Scottish golfing heroes had dried up. Throughout the nineteenth century the Scots had dominated golf. Then English champions began to emerge and now the United States, in the person of Walter Hagen, was taking over the game. Scotland's last champion had been James Braid and he was

Scotsman Ben Sayers, who played in more than 40 British Opens from 1880 to 1923, and Bob Jones at the British Open in 1921.

Bob Jones with the British Open trophy in 1930.

tainted in the eyes of the true patriots, a lapsed Scot, a despised Anglo-Scot who had turned his back on his homeland and settled in England. Scotland ached for a new golfing hero to call its own, even if he could not be one of their own. Initially, Mr. R. T. Jones Jun did not appear as a likely candidate for a new Scottish role model.

On his first visit to Britain in 1921 at the age of 19, Jones made little impression on the sporting public. He was beaten by 6 and 5 in the fourth round of the Amateur Championship at Royal Liverpool by Allan Graham. In the Open championship

> WITHOUT THE WALKER CUP THERE WOULD HAVE BEEN NO GRAND SLAM, NO TICKER TAPE PARADES AND, VERY POSSIBLY, NO AUGUSTA NATIONAL AND NO MASTERS TOURNAMENT.

at St Andrews he took an instant dislike to the Old Course, a common enough reaction on first acquaintance with that wind-swept strip of wasteland. In the third round he took 46 shots to reach the turn. At the short, par-four 10th, which most players see as the best opportunity on the course for a birdie, he took six. At the short 11th, with a green so steeply contoured as to border on the freakish, he still had a tricky putt left after using up five strokes. He said to himself: "What's the use?" and picked up his ball. That, at least, is the way he described it in his book, *Down the Fairway*. When he wrote *Golf is My Game* thirty years later he recounted a slightly different version of this incident. He said he picked up his ball in Hell bunker and put it in his pocket. It is often written that he tore up his card and scattered the pieces on the wind into Eden estuary. That was surely an example of a metaphorical flight of journalistic fancy rather than the literal truth. The fact is he did not return a card for the third round and effectively withdrew from the championship, an incident he was later to regard with the bitterest regret of his entire career. Insofar as the press recorded his exploits, it was to censure his conduct. Strange as it may seem, having put himself out of the championship, he played the fourth round and scored a creditable 72. Another consolation in a generally unsatisfactory baptism of British golf was his commanding form in an unofficial match of American amateurs against a team of home players, an event which proved to be a forerunner of the Walker Cup match.

For the sake of the history of golf it was fortuitous that George Walker did indeed put up a trophy for the encounter which bears his name. Without the Walker Cup there would have been no Grand Slam, no ticker tape parades down Broadway and very

Bob Jones recovers from a bunker at the British Amateur at Hoylake in 1921.

A silver cup commemorating the inaugural Walker Cup Matches held at the National Golf Links of America in 1922.

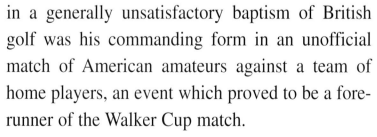

The 1926 Walker Cup Team at St. Andrews: (Front row) Bob Jones, Roland MacKenzie, Jess Sweetser, Francis Ouimet, Watts Gunn. (Back row) Captain Robert Gardner, George Von Elm, Jesse Guilford.

possibly no Augusta National golf club and no Masters tournament. Contrary to the mythology which has grown up around Jones, he was not the scion of a wealthy family. He and Mary lived with his parents in Atlanta because they could not afford a home of their own. He could not even contemplate undertaking an independent golfing foray across the Atlantic; the only possibility for him to compete in the British Amateur and Open championships was to earn his passage by being selected for the American Walker Cup team.

The inaugural match was played at the National Golf Links of America, Long Island, in 1922 and Jones won both his foursomes and singles matches. The following year Jones was not available for the United States team's visit to St Andrews because of university examinations. After the 1924 match at Garden City, New York, it was decided that in the future the fixture should be held in alternate years so it was not until 1926 that Jones was able to return to Britain. He was rather surprisingly beaten in the quarterfinals of the Amateur championship at Muirfield, home of the Honourable Company of Edinburgh Golfers, but the rest of his tour was a triumphal progress of golfing wizardry and unalloyed success.

The Open was played at Royal Lytham and St Annes that year but in those days everyone had to qualify with two rounds over a sectional course. Jones opted to qualify in the southern section, at Sunningdale, close to his favourite London hotel and, perhaps more to the point, the club where his personal club-maker, Jack White, was attached. On the eve of the first qualifying round White delivered a new driver to Jones who promptly named it Jeannie Deans after the Walter Scott heroine. Bobby and Jeannie struck up an immediate rapport and he played what was described at the time as the 'perfect' round of golf. He called it the best competitive round of golf of his life. His score of 66 was near flawless in that he hit every fairway and all but one green in the regulation number of shots, or better. The elation of that extraordinary feat put him in a confident frame of mind as he moved on to Lytham for an Open which was to gleam as one of the brightest highlights in the history of that ancient championship.

At that time they played two rounds on the final day and Jones was two shots off the pace after his third round. Seeking some peace and privacy away from the hurly-burly and glad-handing of the clubhouse, he slipped away into the town for lunch. On his return the gate-keeper demanded to see his ticket. Jones showed him his competitor's badge but that was not enough for the officious idiot whose descendants seem to find regular employment as gate-keepers and car park attendants at British sporting events to this day. Believe it or not, Jones had to buy a ticket in order to get back into the club and win his first British Open.

"Jeannie Deans", Bob's driver.

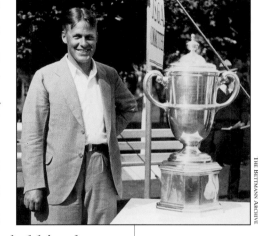

George Herbert Walker donated the Walker Cup.

Below: Bob Jones with the Walker Cup at the Chicago Golf Club in 1928.

Below: The scorecard of the "perfect" qualifying round at Sunningdale in 1926 kept by Jones' chronicler and friend O.B. Keeler.

As noted in *Down The Fairway*, " ... in perfection of execution it stands almost alone: 33 out; 33 back; 33 putts; 33 other shots; not a 2 and not a 5; three strokes under par on each side; only once in trouble and then at no cost. The card shows Mr. Keeler's scoring system, in which the distance of the ball from the pin on reaching the green is noted, in small figures; the putts represented by dots; so it is easy to trace his play."

SUNNINGDALE GOLF CLUB.

Old Course: 6472 Yards.

Par	Holes	Yards		Score		Holes	Yards	
5	1	493	4		5	10	469	4
5	2	454	4		4	11	296	3
4	3	292	4		4	12	443	4
3	4	152	3		3	(13)	175	3
4	5	417	3		5	14	503	4
4	6	418	4		3	15	229	3
4	7	434	4		4	16	426	4
3	8	165	3		4	(17)	422	4
4	9	270	4		4	18	415	4
36		3094	33		36		3378	33
		17						66

The Jones Family

Bob Jones and the great showman Walter Hagen before their match in Sarasota in 1926 for what was billed as "the unofficial championship of the world". Hagen completely dominated Jones for perhaps the only time, winning 10 and 12 over the 36-hole match.

The seventeenth hole at Royal Lytham as it appears today.

Jules Alexander

That was the year that Walter Hagen, ever one for the flamboyant gesture, asked the official scorer to hold the flag on the last green before playing the 150-yard approach shot which, had he holed out with it, would have won him the title. Instead it was Jones, playing behind with his closest rival, Al Watrous, who pulled off the master stroke which was to reverberate around the world. At the long seventeenth he slightly pulled his drive and the ball finished in what today is a formal fairway bunker. At the time it was a wilderness of gorse and heather and Jones' ball lay cleanly on loose sand. Jones made perfect contact with his mashie and the ball soared over all the intervening trouble to plummet into the green. Watrous was so shaken by this miraculous turn of events that he three-putted and lost his lead. Jones won by two strokes and that club now has pride of place among the Lytham club's historic memorabilia. A plaque commemorating that stroke of genius now marks the spot from which it was played.

Jones was now established in the hearts of the British sporting public as a firm favourite. American golf had long been exemplified to the Scots and the English by the swash-buckling braggadocio of Hagen. He was immensely popular, of course, because of his fabulous golf and his outrageous exploits off the course, but it was a showbiz popularity, the way a Barnum and Bailey circus was popular. People smiled and shook their heads when they spoke of Hagen and said: "What a card!" The response to Jones was more human, intimate even; it was a warm embrace of affection.

Jules Alexander

The plaque indicating the approximate location, next to what is now a formal bunker on the 17th hole, where Jones struck the shot that defeated Al Watrous in the 1926 British Open.

The shy smile of Jones, his impeccable manners, his modesty and his sportsmanship struck a chord with the middle class English sporting fraternity in particular because he was the very paradigm of an ideal called the Corinthian ethic. Parents scrimped and saved to send their sons to expensive public schools, less to receive a formal education than to have the Corinthian ethic drummed into them. This involves much more than the tenets of good sportsmanship. It includes such concepts as the game being more important than the player; that you bust a gut to the point of death for your team (or for yourself at golf) but never by a word or gesture betray that you are trying. Hence, practising is tantamount to cheating. Sporting superiority is unworthy unless it is effortless and unrewarded. The gifted amateur is king. The doctrine of the character-building Corinthian ethic is best encapsulated in the smug boast: "The Battle of Waterloo was won on the playing fields of Eton."

Nobody ever had to instruct Jones in the Corinthian ethic. Insofar as he observed its principles, it was inherent in his nature. His tutor, Stewart Maiden, may have guided him in the virtues of patience, perseverance and self-control but it is highly unlikely that a dour Scottish professional would endorse the notion that the state of a match is the most important thing in the world at the time, but, as soon as the match is over, the result is totally irrelevant. After all, Maiden was a Carnoustie man and the 300 immigrant professionals from the tiny Scottish village (pop. 3,000) could hardly have prospered and produced the national champions of seven countries, and champi-ons of every State of the Union, if they held the act of winning to be irrelevant. In any case, men like Charles Blair Macdonald had imported the British conventions of amateur golf when they introduced the game to the United States; so both nations marched to roughly the same tune.

> THE BRITISH FELT JONES TO BE ONE OF THEIR OWN AND THEY REVERED HIM AS MUCH FOR HIS DEPORTMENT AS FOR HIS SKILL.

Besides, Jones had imposed his own version of the Corinthian ethic on himself after a distressing incident early in his career. During a United States Amateur champi-onship the wild youngster ranted and raved on the course and threw a club in self-dis-gust, hitting a woman spectator. He was severely reprimanded and warned that unless he mended his ways he would never again be selected to represent the United States in the Walker Cup team. The contrite Jones reflected on his past boorishness and vowed that henceforth he would never infringe in word or deed the stringent code of sportsmanship he imposed upon him-self. No matter. The British felt Jones to be one of their own and they revered him as much for his deportment as for his skill. And when the Walker Cup match was played at St Andrews there was an added piquan-cy to the emotional bonding of Jones with the Scots because he absolute-ly thrashed the mighty English champion, Cyril Tolley.

Scotland's bloody history must be invoked once again in order to explain the full import of that result. By this time the implacable and well justified hatred in which the Scots held their southern neighbours during the Middle Ages had been sublimated and ritualised and channelled into the substi-tute for war, sport. No sporting occasions in Britain arouse more fulminating passions, both on and off the field of play, than encounters between England and the other three members of the Union: Scotland, Wales and Ireland. Nothing could be more endearing to the Scots than for someone, anyone, to humiliate the English. And that match over the Old Course was a comprehensive dusting by 12 and 11 of the powerful English amateur who drove the 358 yards to the last green at St Andrews three times during one competition.

At the same time another emotional affair was in the brew-ing; Jones was falling deeply and comprehensively in love

Bob Jones and Stewart Maiden in a picture taken by O.B. Keeler at the National Amateur in 1921 at St. Louis. At the time Maiden was the head professional at the St. Louis Country Club.

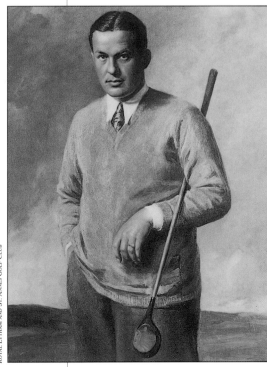

The portrait of Bob Jones that hangs in the clubhouse of the Royal Lytham and St. Annes Golf Club.

with St Andrews and the Old Course. He was later to write: "If I had ever been set down in one place and told I was to play there, and nowhere else, for the rest of my life, I would have chosen the Old Course." And: "In my humble opinion St Andrews is the most fascinating golf course I have ever played." And: "The more I studied it, so that I came to feel that it was for me the most favourable meeting ground possible for an important contest I felt that my knowledge of the course enabled me to play it with patience and restraint until she might exact her inevitable toll from my adversary, who might treat her with less respect and understanding." Jones' growing affection for British golf in general, and St Andrews in particular, communicated itself to the sporting public and was reciprocated a hundredfold.

THE BRITISH SAW HIM AS THE SON THEY MUST ADOPT ... HE REPRESENTED AN UNPRECEDENTED IDEAL OF GOLFING SKILL AND SPORTSMANSHIP.

Jones determined that he must defend his championship, a decision reinforced by the fact that the next year's Open was to be held at St Andrews. With no Walker Cup match to bankroll his visit, he had to scrape together the funds from his own meagre resources. It proved to be a prudent investment. St Andrews welcomed him back with the fervour due to a demigod. Great things were expected of 'King Bobby' and he did not disappoint his loyal subjects. His progress around his beloved Old Course resembled four laps of honour rather than intense competitive golf because nobody could mount anything of a challenge to him. He won by a margin of six strokes with a record championship total of 285.

Surely the most remarkable element in Jones' dominance of world golf was not so much that he was an amateur, for in those days the best amateurs were a match for the leading professionals, but that he was never anything more than an week-end golfer. He would go for months

Bob Jones tees off at the 17th hole of the Old Course at St. Andrews during the 1927 British Open.

without touching a club because his studies demanded his undivided attention. Between winning championships he was also acquiring scholastic honours in mechanical engineering (Georgia Tech), English (Harvard) and the law (Emory). In the home city of one of Europe's oldest universities, whose scarlet-gowned students were a common sight as they cycled furiously through the medieval streets of St Andrews to get in a few holes of golf before classes, the academic prowess of Jones struck an emotional chord.

Jones pitches to the green at St. Andrews.

The following year Jones made up his mind to retire at the end of the 1930 season. That would be a year for the Walker Cup to return to Britain and so it would allow him one more chance to take care of a piece of unfinished business, the winning of the British Amateur championship. It was to be played at St Andrews and we now know how he felt about the place and how he believed it favoured his chances. Another reason for his decision to quit competitive golf was that he knew his friends backed him heavily every time he played. That knowledge offended his principles as an amateur and put an accumulating burden of responsibility onto his shoulders. Besides, it was becoming a matter of considerable urgency that he devote himself fully to his law practice in order to provide for his family.

In the event, despite his affinity for the Old Course, Jones had a desperately tough run in the Amateur championship. In the fourth round he met Tolley and this time the match was no push-over. It proved to be one of the classic matches of this or any other championship, Jones finally being mightily relieved to prevail on the 19th hole. He then had two more narrow squeaks, winning by a single hole, in his progress to a final against the redoubtable Roger Wethered.

For a decade or so the stylish Wethered had been Britain's best amateur. In 1921 only a penalty stroke for accidentally stepping on his own ball had robbed him of the Open Championship. It took intense persuasion to prevail upon him to stay on for a play-off against Jock Hutchison, because he had promised to turn out for his village cricket team. That Corinthian ethic again! Both Wethered and Jones were close to their top form in the final and a thrilling match ended 7 and 6 in Jones' favour. He had now won all four major championships at least once.

Two weeks later he won the Open Championship at Royal Liverpool, meaning that he had won the British Open three times in three attempts. He had conquered Britain as comprehensively as the Roman legions nearly 2,000 years earlier. When Arnold Palmer burst into prominence the matrons of America saw him as the son they wished they'd had. So with Jones, the British saw him as the son they must adopt because he represented an unprecedented ideal of golfing skill and sportsmanship.

So when Jones returned to the United States and won the U.S. Open at Interlachen and the U.S. Amateur championship at Merion, to complete the Grand Slam, his worshipping British fans, and especially the Scots, savoured the vicarious thrill of 'our' Bobby's triumph. It often seems that there is a fundamental difference in the British and American attitudes towards sporting heroes of the past. As a broad generalisation, American heroes fade from the public consciousness whereas in Britain the passing of time inflates the reputations of national heroes. The American passion for statistics rather clouds this distinction because in an unchanging game such as baseball the career records of a Babe Ruth must continue to command respect. But in an evolving game like golf the scoring records of a hundred years ago appear humdrum and someone like Willie Anderson is virtually unknown to contemporary Americans. If

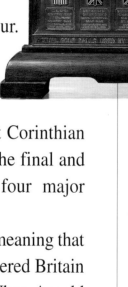

A plaque commemorating the Grand Slam presented to Jones by *Golf Illustrated* (UK) Magazine in 1931.

Anderson had remained in his native Scotland and achieved a similar record of golfing success he would be revered today as a secular saint. So some thirty years after his retirement from competitive golf, the emotional bond between Jones and the Scots was as strong as ever.

> HE LIVES ON, OF COURSE, ... AS THE MAN WHO CONQUERED HIMSELF AND, BY SO DOING CONQUERED GOLF AND ... A NATION.

In 1958 and by now confined to a wheelchair by a debilitating disease, Jones learnt that the inaugural World Amateur Team Championship match would be held in St Andrews that year. He determined to take advantage of that fact and pay what he felt must be his last visit to the city and course which he had come to love so well. He used his influence to get himself appointed as non-playing captain of the American team. The news was conveyed to St Andrews and, before sailing with his team, Jones received a cable from the Town Clerk of St Andrews enquiring whether he would be willing to accept the Freedom of the City of St Andrews. He imagined that this ceremony would involve no more than receiving a token key and cabled his acceptance.

After the Freedom of the City ceremony, Bob Jones and The Lord Provost of St. Andrews.

When he arrived at St Andrews he discovered that the honour being bestowed upon him had traditionally been reserved to a very select band of luminaries of the arts and politics, including only one American, Dr. Benjamin Franklin in 1757. The Younger Hall was packed with civic dignitaries, distinguished golfing personalities, senior academics and well-wishers for the incustion ceremony. The Lord Provost, i.e., mayor of St Andrews, introduced Jones to the assembly and explained some of the privileges of a Burgess and Guild Brothere of the City of St Andrews. They included the rights to cart shells, to take divots (cut turfs) and to dry one's washing upon the first and last fairways of the Old Course. He added: "These are homely terms - and perhaps in an American as well as a British sense - but they may help us to convey to our new Honorary Burgess just what is meant by this freedom ceremony: that he is free to feel at home at St Andrews as truly as in his own home of Atlanta. He is one of our own number, officially now, as he has been for so long unofficially."

When Jones had learnt something of the extent and form of the Freedom ceremony, he had composed a formal acceptance speech. But when he rose to reply he knew, as he later wrote in his autobiography, that he would have no difficulty in finding things to say to the people of St Andrews. His notes remained in his pocket and he spoke from the heart.

The parchment bestowing on Bob Jones the Freedom of the City of St. Andrews.

He recalled his experiences at St Andrews and dwelt in particular on a visit he made to Gleneagles on his way to the Berlin Olympic Games of 1936. On a whim he decided to play a round on the Old Course. He drove over to St Andrews and had lunch and was surprised when he went to the first tee to find a gallery of 2,000 expectant spectators waiting for him. He went out in 32. Several times during his address Jones had to stop and compose the emotions welling up within him.

The silver presentation casket holding the Freedom of the City parchment.

Towards the end he spoke the words that tore at the heart strings of the 1,700 people assembled in the hall: "I could take out of my life everything except my experiences at St Andrews and I would still have a rich, full life." Some accounts reported that Jones shed tears during his address. He did not but, as the Duke of Wellington remarked about the battle of Waterloo, it was damn'd close run thing.

As he and the Lord Provost drove in an electric cart down the aisle the crowd spontaneously roared out the song lamenting the departure into exile of Bonnie Prince Charlie: "Will ye no come back again?" Many people in the hall were openly sobbing. Jones departed, never to return, into the private exile of the wasting disease which was to take his life. He lives on, of course, in legend, especially in St Andrews, as the man who conquered himself and, by so doing, conquered golf and, by so doing, conquered a nation.

Perhaps the feelings of the British people towards Jones can be summarised by a touching incident during that round at St Andrews before the Berlin Olympics. At the short eighth hole he hit a soft, fading four iron around the mound to finish eight feet from the hole and his young Scottish caddy whispered to him: "My, but you're a wonder, Sir!"

That caddie spoke for the entire nation.

Bob Jones tees off on the first hole at St. Andrews in 1936.

LORD BYRON & EMPEROR JONES

BY NICK SEITZ

Byron Nelson's private memory vault is crowded with public treasures, but one of his most cherished memories has nothing to do with his official records for most victories and least stroke average. It was planted during a practice round at the Masters Tournament in the 1940's, when Nelson and Bobby Jones were partners one pastoral spring day against Henry Picard and Gene Sarazen.

Says Nelson, "We all were playing well, including Bob, who was past his heyday but could still strike the ball beautifully. He shot 31 on the back nine that day. It was amazing. During one stretch, starting late on the first nine, they made seven straight birdies—and Jones and I never lost a hole! We played a number of friendly matches together, and I don't believe we ever lost."

Jones and Nelson were a team made for one of those mythical computer tournaments. They wouldn't lose there either. Nelson is the rare legend deserving prominent mention in the same history books with Jones, both having accomplished the unimaginable: Jones' Grand Slam in 1930 and Nelson's 11 straight PGA Tour victories in 1945.

Jones barely played in 1930 beyond the major championships available to him as an amateur, and proved forever peerless at bringing his game to fruition at precisely the right time.

Nelson won a total of 18 tournaments in '45, and posted a stroke average of 68.33. His average in the last round was an even lower 67.88 and, most awesomely of all, a still lower 66.67 in the final round during his 11 consecutive victories. Because it was a war year, Nelson could try for only one major championship, the PGA, and he claimed it.

Lord Byron versus Emperor Jones. The Streak versus The Slam. 1945 versus 1930. The celestial debate was and is as unresolvable as it is stimulating. The two greats were separated by a generation, a gap wider than it might seem because equipment was changing radically as Jones reached the end of his abbreviated career and Nelson began playing for money.

"He won the Grand Slam with the small ball," Nelson says. "It came off the clubface faster, went through the wind better and was easier to putt, but by the same token you got more spin on the large ball and could control it better. People talk about me pioneering the steel shaft. But Bob was the transition player between hickory and steel.

Nelson is given credit for fathering the modern swing, but he deflects some of the credit toward Jones. "I get that because I started using the feet and legs more to keep the clubface square. Bob developed the technique of using the large muscles of the

Byron Nelson compiled one of the finest professional records of all time: 18 tournament victories in 1945, including an almost unbelievable 11 in a row.

Bob Jones and Ben Hogan (seated) with Jimmy Demaret and Byron Nelson at the Masters.

FRANK CHRISTIAN

body. He was looser at the top of the swing than I was, but he had a remarkable ability to control the club. He made a big turn, a very smooth and deliberate turn with lovely rhythm. He was a wonderful woods player, especially fairway woods. He hit them long and straight, and he made a lot of birdies on par-5 holes."

NELSON ... ADMIRES THE DIVERSITY
OF JONES' INTERESTS BEYOND GOLF...

It's no wonder Jones and Nelson were unbeatable partners; their games complemented each other like vintage wine and cheese. Jones was not a pre-eminent long irons player, but Nelson was. Nelson was above average around and on the greens, but Jones was superlative.

"He told me a couple of times he felt the reason I played well in the Masters was that I hit my long irons high and landed them softly," says Nelson. "The boys were complaining recently about how hard the greens were, and I told them—and Picard

FRANK CHRISTIAN

In addition to his mastery of the long irons at Augusta (above), Byron was also a fine putter (below).

and Sarazen who were there agreed with me—that they are not as hard as they used to be. The greens used to be so hard you could hear approach shots bounce on them. I was fortunate to be able to float my iron shots in there, and Bob admired that. But he made up for any relative shortcoming in his game by being a great putter.

"He was a great lag putter, dying the ball at the hole," says Nelson, "and his long, flowing stroke was reminiscent of his full swing. Ben Crenshaw today has that kind of stroke, though not as long as Bob's. But you never saw the clubhead pass his hands. I believe Jones, from 1920 through 1930, holed more good, long putts on the last hole to win major championships than anyone else who ever played golf."

The acutely analytical Paul Runyan, who played with Jones and Nelson in their virtuosic primes, confirms that Jones was less proficient with the long irons and says he was the finest fairway woods striker ever. Runyan remembers playing with Jones in the first Masters and marveling at a long fairway wood shot Jones hit at what was then the 11th hole and is now the second. "He was on the steepest part of the downslope, with the pin behind the right bunker, and he made a nice, supple swing and the ball rose up and up and up and stopped 25 feet above the hole. I told him that was the best spoon or 3-wood shot I had ever witnessed. He said he didn't use a spoon—he used a brassie (2-wood)."

Adds Runyan, "Nelson was magnificent in every category once he remade his swing for the steel shafts, but Bobby was superior, given the equipment he played. He could drive the ball as far as he needed to without giving the appearance of hitting harder."

Runyan agrees that Jones was a world beating putter on fast greens, but says he was much less successful on slow, bumpy greens. "His arm-and-wrist stroke was so smooth but long and less accurate. Even on a six-foot putt his backstroke was twice as long as mine or Byron's."

Nelson met Jones in 1935 when he was first invited to the Masters, largely on the strength of upsetting Lawson

FRANK CHRISTIAN

Little, the king of amateur golf, in the San Francisco Match Play Open, to the delight of his fellow pros who resented having to qualify for the match play field when Little was given a free spot. Nelson's initial impression of Augusta National was surprise at the lack of rough, and he was most impressed with meeting Jones, a folk hero of the era.

"I got acquainted with Bob when we gathered for a group picture out on the front lawn. Later that picture was said to be from the first Masters, but I told them it had to be the second, because I wasn't there in 1934. Actually it was called the Augusta National Invitation until 1939. When we were arranged for the picture, Jones was sitting up in the front and I was tall so I was in the back. Since the tournament was new, he made sure he got to know everyone, and it was a big treat to say hello to him. It was the start of a long, enjoyable relationship with a super, super man."

Bobby Cruickshank checks in at the Masters as Byron Nelson and Ed Dudley look on.

The following spring, 1936, the young Nelson was flattered to notice Jones following him as he played, and took encouragement from the attention. "Knowing his record and popularity, it pleased me to realize he thought I was worth watching. I tied for 12th and won $50, so I wasn't too happy about that, but it made me more determined to get better and perform well in his tournament."

Beginning to master his steel shafts, Nelson performed well enough the next year in his third Masters to win it. He gained six strokes the last day on the leader Ralph Guldahl at the testy 12th and 13th holes, which Nelson played birdie-eagle.

"Bob had some nice comments to make about the way I shot a great 32 on the back nine after starting slowly, and he talked about how I'd shot a course-record 66 the first day, hitting every green in regulation except the par-5 holes which I hit in two. That finishing 32 and his remarks about it did more for my career back then than anything, because I realized my game could hold up under pressure. I'd led, lost the lead and finished well. There was no green jacket for the winner in those days, but it was a great thrill to have Bob present me the gold medal. I still have it, and it still reminds me of the most important win of my career, the one that gave me confidence in myself."

Nearly as thrilled was a group of leisure gamblers known as the Greek Syndicate that had purchased Nelson in a local Calcutta pool popular at the time.

It was that '37 Masters that inspired O. B. Keeler, Jones' Boswell, to dub the winner "Lord Byron" after a poem the original Lord Byron wrote about Napoleon at Waterloo. The latter-day Lord Byron found it ironic that his namesake drank himself to death at an early age while he himself abstained.

After Nelson's first two Masters Tournaments, his cumulative score astonishingly stayed in red numbers, signifying that he was under par, for more than 900 holes. In 1938 Jones maintained a young tradition by pairing himself with the defending champion in the first round, a Masters hallmark that endures today in the form of pairing the defender with the U.S. Amateur champion on opening day. Nelson remembers Jones as being enjoyable to play with, chatting just enough and offering encouragement to the younger man. In his role as tournament host, Jones also played the last round with the leader, and when he was too ill to continue playing in the mid-1940s, he asked Nelson to take his place the final day.

Says Nelson, "It was a great honor, and I played with the leader from 1946 until '56, when Ken Venturi and I would have been paired and it was agreed that since I was his mentor there might be some advantage to him even though he wouldn't be asking me any questions. The Masters has always wanted to keep everything totally proper. Before then I played with seven winners. After 1956 they began pairing by scores. That practice started at Augusta, I believe, like so many other things."

Nelson finished fifth in 1938, and established nearly permanent residency in the Masters top 10, running third in 1940 and second in '41 before winning again in 1942, over Ben Hogan in a ding-dong playoff that is the grand climax I most wish I'd seen. The two proud Texans who grew up in the same hardscrabble caddieyard leading up to the Depression were hard to impress, but they took due note that all the pros who could stay for the playoff were in the gallery, two dozen of them Nelson estimates.

A regal, commanding presence today despite a hip transplant and ensuing complications, Nelson might have stepped out of Mount Rushmore, so firmly chiseled are his strong, full features. His voice is unwavering, his mind fully apprehending. He remembers the 1942 Hogan playoff shot for shot.

"I was a little nervous and tight at the start, as everybody was playing Hogan, he was such a great player, and on the first hole I hit a bad drive into the trees and made a double bogey. I bogeyed number 4 and now I was three shots down. But I'd settled down, and from 6 through 13 I went six under par, playing the best golf of my career, and I shot 69 and he shot 70." Nelson clearly recalls Jones' comments afterward. "He said it was wonderful how I'd turned my game around a hundred percent and how difficult that was to do. He said to me privately that I played so well and so differently from the way he had played that he couldn't identify with it. He was so diplomatic he wouldn't have said that in front of Ben at the ceremony, because it would have detracted from how well Ben played. You can imagine what that meant for me to have him say that."

Jones became a model of diplomacy and sportsmanship, but Nelson occasionally saw a tougher, flintier side of the quintessential Southern gentleman. "One time at the dinner for the Masters champions the players were complaining about the way the pin had been placed on the third hole, saying it was almost impossible to make a birdie. Bob spoke up and said, 'You guys make me sick. You think you're supposed to birdie every hole. There are going to be some hole placements out there where if you want a birdie you're really going to have to earn it.' He could be very stern—polite but stern."

Nelson was struck by Jones' knowledge of golf history and technique, couched in lucid, literate commentary. "He was very articulate, and wrote many fascinating arti-

Amateur Ken Venturi led through three rounds of the 1956 Masters.

Ben Hogan drives from the first tee as his playing partner Byron Nelson watches.

cles and books on the game. When he spoke, everyone paid good attention."

Nelson, a man of commendably straightforward tastes, openly admires the diversity of Jones' interests beyond golf, ranging from the literature of Fielding to the arias of Puccini. "He was highly educated, but he didn't flaunt it," Nelson says.

Coincidentally I have been picking my way through Willard Sterne Randall's careful biography of Jefferson, whose breadth of interests, when he wasn't occupied with inventing a nation, extended from practicing law and architecture to hiring domestic help that could double as talent for his dream of fielding his own symphony orchestra. Jones, the more I learn of him, approached that kind of mental diversity more than any other athlete I can think of. He came the closest, as Herb Wind put it, to being a great man in the full sense of the term: "Like Winston Churchill, he had the quality of being at the same time much larger than life and exceedingly human."

As Nelson says, Jones didn't flaunt his cultured tastes, and most of the time was quiet company. But behind the quiet was a towering wall of self-discipline. "Later in his life, when his crippling disease kept getting worse, you knew he had to be bitter about it, but he never let it show. Even when you went down to visit with him at his cabin at Augusta National, and someone would have to light his cigarette for him and that sort of thing, he never complained. He always seemed more interested in how you were doing and what you had to say."

I gained an appreciation for that largeness of spirit in 1966, when I covered the Masters for the first time, for a newspaper in Oklahoma City, and subsequently returned home to write about the winner Jack Nicklaus and his chances of winning the modern Grand Slam. My two most vivid and fond memories of the tournament were seeing Jones on the course in a golf cart and seeing Nelson play, it being a Jones master touch to include past winners in the field for as long as they felt they were able to perform. Nowhere else could I have seen the great Nelson compete for a first and only time.

Honorary Masters starters: Sam Snead, Gene Sarazen and Byron Nelson with Masters Chairman Jack Stephens.

I did not get to meet Jones, but a few weeks later, in a flash of youthful audacity, placed a call to him at his Atlanta office. To my surprised delight, he came on the phone, and we conversed for the better part of a half hour about his Grand Slam and Nicklaus' goal of succeeding it. Savaged by illness, he sounded hoarse, but his thought process was icepick sharp, and he gave me more than enough material.

"I felt the strain most when I was going for the fourth leg of the Slam," he said, "mainly because I knew I never was going to play those four tournaments again in one year. I played them all only once every four years, when the Walker Cup team went to Great Britain. That's the only time I would compete in the British Amateur—I only played in it three times."

He recalled that friends of his put up S50 at 50-1 odds with Lloyd's of London that he would win his Slam in 1930. "They wanted to put up more, but Lloyd's limited its liability to $2,500, so my friends didn't make as much as they might have."

In more modern times, Lloyd's declined to insure against Nicklaus or anyone else winning the modern Grand Slam. The insurance giant need not worry. The Slam — and The Streak will endure.

AN ENDURING LEGACY

BY LARRY DORMAN

*I*t is possible to think of Bob Jones without thinking of Augusta National and the Masters. After all, there were all those other accomplishments. There was the Grand Slam of 1930. There were those ticker-tape parades in New York and there were the 23 tournament victories in a 13-year competitive career that ended when he was just 28 years old. It is not at all possible, though, to think of the Masters and Augusta National without thinking of Jones.

He breathed life into Augusta National and he is the very soul of the Masters, then and now.

The indelible imprint of Jones is everywhere at the Augusta National. It is on the golf course itself, which he co-designed with Dr. Alister Mackenzie. It is on the golf tournament every spring, a tournament so well-conceived and run that it is the standard by which all other golf competitions are measured.

A young Bob Jones and a young Cliff Roberts before the founding of the Augusta National Golf Club.

It is in the manor clubhouse and in all the cabins that stand in silent testimony to his vision, in the cases of the trophy room, and on the wall of the Jones Cabin, where a portrait hangs of a young Bob Jones, his hair slicked and parted and his smooth, unlined face smiling. That portrait of the artist as a young man was painted by Dwight D. Eisenhower when he was the president of the United States.

Jones is as intertwined with the clay soil of Augusta as the giant roots of the great oak trees. His spirit lives in the towering pines, and there is a palpable sense of him in every corner of the place, each spring, when his dream comes back to life during Masters week.

To this day, the tournament is a reflection of all that Jones loved about the game. One could only imagine the joy Jones would have felt over the presence of the sensational young amateur, Tiger Woods, at his first Masters in 1995. That an amateur could command so much attention and cause so much commotion with his golf game is something that definitely would have brought a smile to Jones' face. His inclusion of a representative sprinkling of amateurs in the Masters field was another master stroke. It gave us one of Augusta's greatest shows, when Billy Joe Patton, the lumber executive from Morgantown, North Carolina, darn near won the Masters back in 1954. Billy Joe, the lifetime amateur, for-

President Eisenhower presents his portrait of Bob Jones to Bob at Augusta National.

Amateur Billy Joe Patton and Bob Jones at the Masters in 1954.

FRANK CHRISTIAN

ever endeared himself to Jones with his gambling style, a go-for-broke manner that left him one thin stroke out of a playoff with Samuel Jackson Snead and Ben Hogan.

This was the sort of thing Jones envisioned, an amateur taking on the finest pro-

> "No MAN LEARNS TO DESIGN A GOLF COURSE SIMPLY BY PLAYING GOLF, NO MATTER HOW WELL."

fessionals, and young Tiger Woods hitting the greens at par-five holes with short irons would have, one is certain, fit right into the original concept.

The first time he laid eyes on the property, Jones knew. He was standing on the lawn out-side the old manor clubhouse, looking down across the sweeping vistas toward the valley that would become golf's most famous corner of the world. Already, he could hear the roars, see the misery and the elation, feel the exquisite drama of the golf tournament that would come to define his life just as surely as his playing career had.

The visionary in Jones saw it unfold. On a December day as he stood with his friend Clifford Roberts, the man who first conceived the idea of Augusta National, Jones was gripped by the special place that ultimately would become the home of the Masters. It was as though it had all been preordained. That hallowed hollow that would be Amen Corner, sitting untouched then down by the creek, was beckoning.

Intuitively, Jones sensed something grand, right at that moment. It was the winter of 1930 and his competitive career was over. Now, with Father Time's chill breeze on his cheek, Jones knew there was something more to be done, something that would become as synonymous with the name Bob Jones as the Grand Slam.

RALPH W. MILLER LIBRARY

"When I walked out on the grass terrace under the big trees behind the house and looked down over the property," Jones would write later, "the experience was unforget-table. It seemed that this land had been lying here for years just waiting for somebody to lay a golf course upon it. Indeed, it even looked as though it already were a golf course."

JULES ALEXANDER

Perhaps the most photographed hole in the world, the beauti-ful par-five 460-yard thirteenth at Augusta National.

After Jones' defeat in the 1929 U.S. Amateur, he visited neighboring Cyprus Point Golf Club that had just opened. It is understood that it was here that Jones decid-ed on Alistair Mackenzie as the architect for his dream course since he was so impressed with the work he did at Cyprus Point. Jones is pictured here with the Cyprus Point golf professional.

The 365 acres that lay at his feet, once a nursery owned by the Belgian immi-grant family of Baron Prosper Jules Alphonse Berckmans, would become a golf course, all right. The land, which had lain fallow for about 15 years before its discovery by Roberts, would be transformed into the most-pho-tographed, most-discussed, most-emulated American golf course of the last half cen-tury. In earlier times, Indians had camped there. Local historians believe that De Soto and his explorers had crossed it in search of the Mississippi.

Now, hundreds of years later, Bob Jones and Clifford Roberts would transform it forever. They found a golf course architect who agreed with their vision. The man was Dr. Alister Mackenzie, a Scot who not only shared Jones' passion for the game and his vision for design, but his philosophy as well. Both men were, as Jones

wrote in his book, *Golf Is My Game*, "extravagant admirers of the Old Course at St. Andrews." And so they decided that this new Augusta National — purchased at the hardly extravagant price of $70,000 — would be, with obvious variations but as nearly as possible, an inland version of that seaside links that is the cradle of the game.

Mackenzie was the ideal choice. The former practicing physician was considered the best architect of his day. On top of that he had the good sense to accept the input from Jones, the best player of his day. "I think Mackenzie and I managed to work as a completely sympathetic team," Jones wrote. "Of course, there was never any question that he was the architect and I his advisor and consultant. No man learns to design a golf course simply by playing golf, no matter how well."

But Jones had formed a certain view, that the purpose of any golf course should be "to give pleasure, and that to the greatest possible number of players, without respect to the capabilities." In other words, he knew that this new golf course, this Old Course in the new world, would have to strike a balance, to challenge the skilled player and not crush the spirit of the high-handicapper. He and Mackenzie created just such a masterpiece.

Bob Jones and construction engineer Wendell P. Miller direct the activity during the building of the golf course at Augusta National.

Mackenzie had designed more than 50 golf courses, but when he was done with this one, when it first opened for play in December of 1932, he proclaimed it "my best opportunity and, I believe, my finest achievement." It could very well be. Although he never lived to see the first Masters played there in 1934, he did experience the positive reactions from the opening.

There were just 29 sand traps on the course, a welcome departure from the bunker mentality prevalent in those days. Jones and Mackenzie rightly theorized that bunkers generally affect only the unskilled player, and that player already is penalized enough — by virtue of his lack of skill. The fairways were wide and rough was virtually nonexistent.

The golf course is inviting to players of all ability. But when springtime comes and April approaches, Augusta National becomes the consummate test, a hard and fast examination of every facet of the game and the psychological makeup of the best players in the world.

Bob Jones hits tee shots on what is now the eighth hole at Augusta National. To Bob's right is Alistair Mackenzie and to his right is Cliff Roberts.

It becomes the Masters.

When Cliff Roberts first suggested that name, Jones rejected it. Too presumptuous, he said. The whole idea for staging a tournament had grown out of discussions with the United States Golf Association about the possibility of staging a U.S. Open at Augusta, and when that was deemed to be impossible because the summer weather would be unsuitable for optimum golf course setup, the idea for an invitational tournament was born.

In 1934, the first Augusta National Invitation

Tournament was played. Although he had not played competitively in four years, and despite his initial resistance to the idea, Jones agreed to play. That decision sealed the tournament's destiny. Roberts knew that any chance the tournament had to become one of golf's prominent events was dependent on Jones' presence.

Roberts' insistence was driven by pragmatic considerations. Ever the bottom line man, he knew exactly what Jones meant to a field. Roberts wrote about it in *The Story of the Augusta National Golf Club*.

"Some of those who took part in the discussions were afraid that the best players might not all respond to an invitation without Bob being a participant," Roberts recalled. "I particularly was concerned about gate receipts without the enormous drawing power of Bob as a contestant. In 1930 the U.S. Open with Bob in the field established a record of $23,382 in gate receipts. In 1931, without Bob, the sale of tickets dropped to $12,700.

> AS GENTEEL AND URBANE AS JONES WAS, HE COULD BE AN UNNERVING PRESENCE, EVEN LONG AFTER HIS PLAYING DAYS WERE DONE ...

"It was therefore plain to see that our gate receipts might easily be twice as large if Bob played than if he did not."

As difficult as it might be to imagine today's Masters committee being concerned with the gate — other than with how many people it will regrettably have to turn away from it — that was the situation then. And so Jones decided he would accede to Roberts' wishes, and he would play in the tournament. It was not an easy decision for him. He had been absent from competition for four years, and even though he had been playing well in matches with his friends, he was concerned that his play would neither be up to his own standards nor to the rather unrealistic expectations of his legion of fans.

"It was one thing to drive and play iron shots as well as before," Jones wrote in his book, "but quite another to reacquire the delicate touch and confidence around the green which was so necessary on this course. None of the informal golf I had played around Atlanta, or even at the Augusta National, had been played on greens anything like those at Augusta in tournament condition. I soon found there was a great deal of difference."

One thing, though, was very much the same. The aura of Jones was undiminished. His return to competitive golf was the front page news, all across the country. Every one of the players he invited to the tournament showed up, and some who weren't invited came to spectate. And another thing was just as it always had been: Jones was nervous. His nerve-endings were always jangled during competition, and now the prospect of playing in what amounted to the most glittering field of the year was sinking in.

Bob Jones putts on the ninth green during the 1935 Masters as Horton Smith looks on.

A famous foursome: Bob Jones drives off the first tee at Augusta National during a practice round at the Masters as Tommy Armour, Walter Hagen and Gene Sarazen look on.

FRANK CHRISTIAN

Bob Jones and
Paul Runyon at the
1934 Masters.

There was a spot on the side of the middle finger of his right hand that always callused. When the callus split, as it often did, Jones had to wrap it in tape. The morning of his first round of the first Masters, Jones went through the pre-round ritual.

"I noticed as I wrapped this finger before going to the tee that my hands were trembling a bit," Jones later recalled in *Golf is My Game*. "And I felt the familiar, vacant sensation in my stomach."

Those sensations were not worrisome to Jones, since they usually meant he would play well. After all, he had rarely done otherwise. But his concerns about returning to competition were well founded. In the 11 times he played in the Masters, Jones never finished better that the tie for 13th he managed in the inaugural event.

Jones quickly realized he would not be the golfer he was. The nines were reversed for that first tournament — Roberts switched them to their present configuration immediately afterward, when he had noticed that the light was better on the present back nine later in the day — and Jones played the first four holes in 1 under par. Still, he felt uneasy with his putting stroke, and he wasn't certain about his concentration.

He was paired with Paul Runyan, who was the leading scorer and leading money winner from the previous year. As Jones stepped to the fifth tee, which is now the 14th, he was concerned that the nervousness that used to leave him within a hole or two was still there. Distracted by the whirring of a motion picture camera, he stepped away from the ball. He then hurried his setup, hit his drive before he was ready, and pushed the ball into the right trees.

"At that very instant," he recalled, "I realized that this return to competition was not going to be too much fun. I realized, too, that I simply had not the desire nor the willingness to take the punishment necessary to compete in that kind of company. I think I realized, too, that whatever part I might have in the Masters Tournament from then on would not be as a serious contender."

As usual, Jones was correct. He never was a serious contender. He shot 76 on that chilly March day, then 72, a score he managed six times in 44 competitive rounds at Augusta National. He never shot lower than 72. His stroke average for all 11 Masters appearances was 75.93, and he stopped playing after the 1948 tournament after closing rounds of 79-79.

FRANK CHRISTIAN

Jimmy Demaret,
Lloyd Mangram,
Bob Jones and
Charlie Yates.

Says Charles Yates, the fine player who was low amateur in five of the first 11 Masters: "Bob would never admit to this, I'm sure, but I know that because he was the official host, and wanted to make everybody feel welcome, he would stop and speak to all these friends and admirers of his who had come out to the tournament. I think maybe he lost some of his concentration."

He might have. But he never lost the estimation of his peers. Runyan recalled that while Jones obviously wasn't the dominant player in the Masters he had been during his competitive career, he was still a presence who was held in something approaching awe by his fellow golfers.

In a 1989 interview, Runyan talked about the affect Jones had on other players. "It seemed to me that when Bobby was playing in the professional events, most of us played like we had handcuffs on. We didn't want to lose to an amateur, you see. We didn't want to have to admit that an amateur was the best player in the world at that time."

But Runyan, whose best Masters finish was third in the 1942 tournament, concedes that the Jones of 1930 was, indeed, the best player in the world, pro or amateur. During his association with him at the Masters he came to appreciate what it was that set Jones apart as a ball striker. Bob's putting and chipping might have left him after his retirement, but he remained one of the great ball strikers in the game until his illness.

> EACH YEAR IN THE SPRING, THE TOURNAMENT THAT LIVES IN HIS IMAGE COMES TO LIFE.

Runyan's analysis of Jones' action bears repeating: "He had a very big pivot. He was strong. He had a strength that was more fluid than quick. It had a very long duration of application. He's got the biggest pivot of them all. He made a full 90-degree hip turn.

"If he was playing a 380-yard, par-four hole, his swing went back to about horizontal, a nice rubbery swing, and the ball went down the fairway about 230, 240 yards, usually bullet-straight, neither hooking nor slicing. He had a change of pace that was just fabulous. If he was playing a 425-yard hole, that stroke just dipped on down another 10 or 15 inches with the same timing the ball went 265 or 270. If he was playing a 535-yard, par-five hole, it would just dip back there a little farther and with the same motion the ball went 300 yards — with hickory shafts! He was very long."

As genteel and urbane as Jones was, he could be an unnerving presence, even long after his playing days were done and even to players whose stature would one day equal his. This was something that all of the professionals of his day would talk about, often over stiff drinks with the great man himself. They used to tell Jones, only half-jokingly, that they were glad he retired when he did, since they didn't much like their chances, day-in and day-out, against him. Snead, Hogan, Jimmy Demaret, these were some of the multiple Masters winners who always spoke in reverential tones about Jones and his contribution to the game and his ability on the golf course. The letters to Jones from tournament winners invariably were testimonials.

"Jones was one of the greatest ball strikers who ever lived," Snead once said, "but as fine a player as he was, he was even more impressive as a man." Jack Nicklaus, who grew up at Scioto Country Club, was in awe of Jones because of the tales about what Jones had done at Scioto during his 1926 U.S. Open victory there. Nicklaus tells two stories about how encounters with his childhood hero left him daunted and a little embarrassed.

The first occurred during the 1955 United States Amateur at the Country Club of Virginia. It was the 15-year old Nicklaus' first encounter with Jones, who was watching him play the 460-yard finishing hole. Even then, Nicklaus was very long. He hit a long-iron into the

(Back Row) Gary Player, Jack Nicklaus, Arnold Palmer and amateur A. Downing Gray. Bob Jones and Cliff Roberts are seated.

Bob Jones and
Harry Cooper at the
1934 Masters.

green. Jones was impressed.

"Young man," Jones said, "I've been out here quite awhile there have only been a couple of people today who reached this green in two You're one of them. I'm going to come and watch you play a few holes tomorrow."

The next day Nicklaus was 1-up through 10 holes in his match with Bob Gardner. As he was walking to the 11th tee, he saw a cart coming down the 10th fairway. In it was Bob Jones. Nicklaus promptly went bogey-bogey-double bogey and lost all three holes to go 2 down. Jones turned to Charlie Nicklaus.

"He said to my dad, 'I don't think I'm doing Jack any good,'" Nicklaus recalled. "And that was my introduction to Bob Jones."

That was Jones first look at the man who would dominate his Masters tournament like no one in history. It was quite a different scene by the 18th green at Augusta National 10 years later, when Nicklaus had set the scoring record of 271 and Jones issued the memorable line, "He plays a game with which I am not familiar."

Only a year earlier, Nicklaus also had played a game with which Jones was not familiar, when he hit the worst shot of his career and nearly injured his hero. This was his other humbling encounter with Jones. It happened at Augusta's 12th hole, when Nicklaus was chasing Arnold Palmer and had closed to within a couple of shots. Jones was sitting in his cart and Cliff Roberts was standing next to him to

Sam Snead and
Bob Jones at the
1954 Masters.

the right of the tee over near where a TV tower now stands. Nicklaus took back his 8-iron and swung, and the ball went right off the hosel of the club, dead right.

"I just cold shanked it," Nicklaus said. "I almost hit them. I went over there and nobody ever said one word. He never said a word. I never said a word.

"It was more than a little embarrassing."

Bob Jones didn't live to see Jack Nicklaus win the fourth of his six Masters titles in 1972. The disease that had sapped his physical strength, but never his mind, for the last 20 years of his life claimed him in December of 1971. But he will never be gone from the Masters. Each year in the spring, the tournament that lives in his image comes to life. Under the huge oak tree behind the manor clubhouse, those who were fortunate enough to know him swap tales about his capacity for corn liquor and his love of a good off-color joke, of his uncanny genius with a golf club and the dignity with which he dealt with success and failure, with the best of fortune and the worst.

Only such a man could inspire the lasting loyalties that Jones did. A resolution written in 1966 when the club stockholders got together for their annual meeting sums it all up. At the behest of Cliff Roberts, Jones would be named president in perpetuity of the Augusta National Golf Club. He would have objected, but he would have been shouted down. The resolution tells you why.

"It has been well and truly said that every great institution is the lengthened shadow of a man. So it is with the Augusta National Golf Club: the man being Robert Tyre Jones, Jr."

THE FIRST BIG WIN

Since he burst on the golf scene at age 14 in the 1916 U.S. Amateur at Merion, Bob Jones had developed into what many considered to be the best shot maker in the game. Journalists referred to him as the "boy wonder." But Bob had yet to win any of the big national tournaments.

The 1923 Open at the Inwood Country Club, a links-like course on the outskirts of New York City, was Bob's eleventh start in a major championship. All of the top stars of the day were there: Gene Sarazen, the defending champion, Walter Hagen — the 1914 and 1919 champion, Joe Kirkwood, Bobby Cruickshank, Johnny Farrell, Leo Diegel, "Wild Bill" Melhorn and Macdonald Smith for the professionals and Chick Evans — Open champion in 1916 and Francis Ouimet — the 1913 winner, and the 21-year-old Bob Jones for the amateurs.

His game coming into the Open was not sharp — he had spent the past year immersed in his studies at Harvard and had played very little golf. To remedy this he convinced his teacher Stewart Maiden, the head professional at his club in Atlanta, to come to Long Island. But during the practice rounds, his golf seemed to get worse, not better.

Yet with the beginning of the tournament, Bob's golf suddenly rounded into tournament shape.

In the first round Jones was paired with Walter Hagen and shot a 71, finishing one shot behind the leader, Jock Hutchison. In the second round Jones had 73 for a 144 total at the halfway point, while Hutchison had 72 for a 142, leaving Bob two strokes shy. Bobby Cruickshank was third with 145. Inwood was indeed playing tough for the National Open as there were only three other scores under 150 after two rounds.

Bob Jones on Inwood's 17th tee.

☞ Jones drives on the 16th as Gene Sarazen, the defending U.S. Open Champion, watches.

FINISHING LIKE A YELLOW DOG

With two rounds played on the last day, second round leader Jock Hutchison soared to an 82 and Bobby Cruickshank shot a 78. Bob Jones, paired with Gene Sarazen for the last day's double round, played his first nine in a disappointing 41, but he came back with a 35, giving him a lead of three shots over Cruickshank and four over Hutchison.

Jones once again began the outward nine with sloppy play: he sliced his tee shot at the opening hole and made bogey; he hooked his tee shot at the par-three seventh for a double bogey 5 and made the turn in 39, against a par of 37. He played the next six holes in two under par, but pulled his second shot out of bounds on the sixteenth, yet still managed a bogey. On 17 he made another bogey. On the 425 yard par-four 18th he hooked his second into the crowd, leaving him with a difficult pitch over a bunker. He hit it heavy, landed in the bunker and made a double bogey 6 for a 76.

As he left the 18th green, O.B. Keeler told Jones he thought he had won. Jones replied "I didn't finish like a champion. I finished like a yellow dog."

Cruickshank, playing an hour and a half behind Jones, double bogeyed the 16th, but hit it to five feet on 18 and made the putt for birdie to force a playoff for the National Open title.

☞ Jones extricates himself from the sand.

Inset: Bob Jones pitches out of the sand to the 18th green.

Bob Jones putting during the playoff round as Cruickshank looks on.

THE PLAYOFF

The playoff started the next day under overcast skies in front of a crowd of 10,000. Although only three of the first 17 holes were halved, they were all even on the 18th tee. Cruickshank hit first and pulled his tee shot onto a road behind a tree, leaving himself with no shot at the pond fronted green; all he could do was play short of the water.

Jones hit his tee shot in the right rough about 200 yards from the green. With Maiden looking on, he promptly hit a 2-iron off a bare lie eight feet from the pin. This approach shot proved to be one of the finest of Jones' career.

Cruickshank's third shot went over the green and it took him three to get down.

Bob finally won the big one. His first thought was, "I don't care what happens now, I had won a championship."

Bobby Cruickshank prior to the start of the playoff with Jones.

THE SPOILS OF VICTORY

O n his return from the big victory at Inwood, O.B. Keeler reported that Atlanta "...put on the first of many tremendous welcomes, with a band and a parade which wound up at the Chamber of Commerce so the mayor and various prominent citizens could make speeches about Bobby, who was terribly embarrassed."

Top: The first of four times Bob received the Open trophy.

Above: Atlanta gave Bob a rousing welcome home after his first U.S. Open victory.

Bob Jones at the 1923 U.S. Open trophy presentation ceremony.

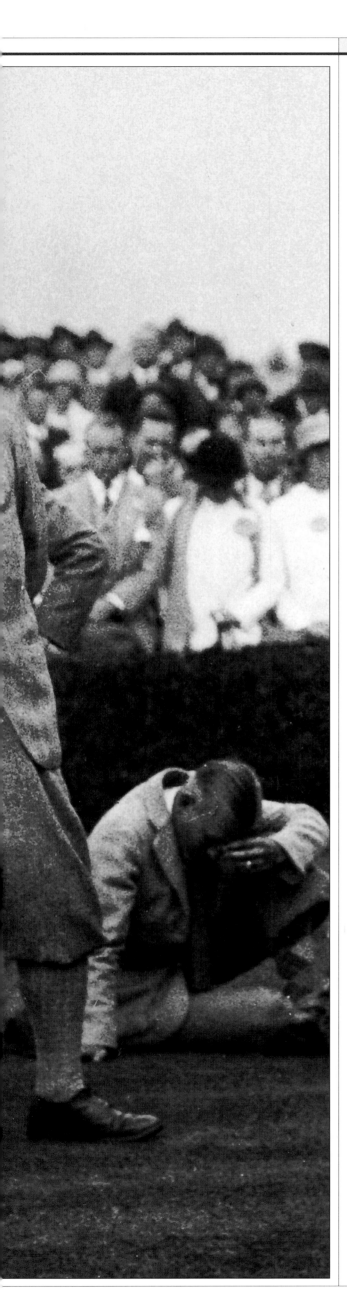

"Old Man Par"

Recently married and having received his degree from Harvard, Jones played well in his defense of the U.S. Open at Oakland Hills near Detroit, finishing second to slightly built Cyril Walker. Now it was on to the scene of his debut in national competition as a youngster of just 14 in kneepants, at the Merion Cricket Club outside of Philadelphia.

Three rounds that Jones played in - one at the '23 Open and the other two at the '24 Amateur - led Bob to a method of approaching competition that would serve him well for the remainder of his career. He concluded that he needed to concentrate on playing against the par listed on the scorecard - "Old Man Par" he called it - rather than his opponent. (The first time Jones had any inkling of playing against an unseen opponent was when, as an eleven year old, he watched Harry Vardon play in a series of exhibition matches in Atlanta.)

The first incident occurred at the 1923 Open when Bob tried to figure what score he needed to win based on what his main competitors had shot. By playing against a score he thought he needed to shoot in the final, rather than the scorecard, he almost dissipated his chances. As Jones later said, "What I should have done, of course, was to set my sights on par and shoot for that as best I could and shut out of my mind Bobby Cruickshank and Jock Hutchinson and the rest of them." Fortunately, he won in a playoff against Cruickshank.

In the 1923 Amateur at the Flossmoor Jones tied with Chick Evans for the medal in the qualifying rounds and they decided to play it off. Jones shot a two-under par 70 to Evan's four-over 76. Once again he realized the inherent correctness of playing against par and not his opponent.

After the '23 Amateur, Jones stood by his newly adopted philosophy of aggressively battling "Old Man Par" and not his opponent. From that point on, Bob Jones was only defeated three times in match play and then, only when his opponent had a hot round relative to par.

In the semi-finals of the 1924 U.S. Amateur, Jones was disturbed that he had to face his old friend Francis Ouimet. At the time Jones told O.B. Keeler, "I don't want to play Francis. I'm going well, and his game is all shot to pieces, and I'm pretty sure I can beat him, and darn it all — I don't want to beat him". In no uncertain terms, O.B. told him to play the card of the course - "Old Man Par" - and not Ouimet. And that is precisely what Jones did, soundly beating Ouimet 11-and-10, the worst defeat in Ouimet's career.

In the final he faced George Von Elm, one of the elite amateurs of the day. Nevertheless, Jones finished the match on the 10th hole in the afternoon round by a score of 10-and-8, thus realizing his greatest ambition, winning the United States Amateur Championship.

After five consecutive top-ten finishes in the U.S. Open - including two seconds and one victory, and now a resounding win in the U.S. Amateur - to go along with his record of achieving no less than the semi-final round in each of the five U.S. Amateurs played since its resumption after World War I, "major championship golf (was) from this point until his retirement", Herbert Warren Wind wrote in *The Story of American Golf*, "... the chronicle of Jones versus the field".

Prior to the start of play at the 1924 U.S. Amateur, Jones, Von Elm and several USGA officials pose with three of the USGA's trophies: (left to right) the Walker Cup, the U.S. Amateur trophy and the Women's Amateur trophy, the most handsome of all of the USGA's trophies.

◄ Jones with the original U.S. Amateur trophy.

TWO IN A ROW

akmont Country Club, just outside of Pittsburgh, with its multitude of hazards and diabolically furrowed bunkers, was the venue for the 1925 U.S. Amateur. It was here in 1919 that Jones, as a young lad of 17, finished second in just his second attempt in the Amateur.

In an effort to create greater interest and speed-up the competition, the USGA changed the format from a series of 18-hole matches among 32 qualifiers and a 36-hole final to one incorporating just 16 qualifiers playing 36-hole matches.

Winning his early matches by scores of 11-and-10, 6-and-5, and 7-and-6, Bob Jones had a relatively easy time leading up to the final.

Watts Gunn, a Jones protégé from Georgia Tech who Bob Jones encouraged to enter the tournament, played extremely well, ending-up in the final against his mentor. It was the first and only time that two members from the same club had ended-up in the finals of the Amateur.

Through the first 12 holes of the final match Jones was one down to the younger Gunn but, in a burst of inspired play over the next eight holes, Bob had relatively short putts on each green and went six up on his fellow Atlantan. Jones finished the match on the 29th green, winning 8-and-7.

Bob Jones had successfully defended his Amateur Championship for the first time.

Top: Bob Jones warms-up outside the Oakmont clubhouse.

Above: Bob Jones and Watts Gunn with the U.S. Amateur trophy. The trophy was destroyed in a fire several months later at East Lake.

☞ Jones defeated Watts Gunn 8 and 7 in the final of the 1925 U.S. Amateur at Oakmont.

THE FIRST BIG VICTORY
IN BRITAIN

After a fifth round defeat by unknown Andrew Jamieson in the British Amateur at Muirfield and the American victory in the Walker Cup Matches at St. Andrews, Bob Jones had booked passage to the United States. However, not wanting to appear unsportsmanlike after the loss in the Amateur, he entered the British Open at Royal Lytham and St. Anne's on England's west coast.

Qualifying at Sunningdale, he shot an incredibly symmetrical 66 — considered by many to be the finest round ever played in Great Britain, and followed the next day with a 68 to win the qualifying medal by a whopping seven strokes.

After the first round Jones was four strokes behind leader Walter Hagen's 68; in the second round he added another 72 leaving him tied for the lead with professional Bill Melhorn at 144.

Top: Three masters of British golf with a young Bob Jones at the 1926 British Open at Royal Lytham and St. Annes, Ted Ray, James Braid and Harry Vardon.

Above: Bob Jones putts at the home hole at Royal Lytham as seen from the clubhouse.

☞ Bob Jones out of the sand at Royal Lytham.

"... THE GREATEST SHOT IN THE HISTORY OF BRITISH GOLF."

Paired with American professional Al Watrous in the last two rounds, Bob shot a 73 to Watrous's 69, leaving him two back of leader Watrous entering the final 18. Putting erratically, Jones was still two behind with five holes to play. With pars at the fourteenth and fifteenth holes to Watrous's three putt bogeys at each hole, Jones was now even with three holes to play. Both parred the sixteenth.

All even on the seventeen, Watrous split the fairway with his drive. Jones hooked his tee shot onto a sandy area — not quite the formal bunker it is today, on the left side of the fairway where it doglegs to the left about 175 yards from the green. First to play, Watrous, undoubtedly feeling the pressure of being in contention for a major championship, hit a weak shot to the front edge of the green. Bob, faced with a blind shot off of sand to a rock-hard green, selected a mashie-iron — about a strong 4-iron in today's nomenclature. He proceeded to pick the ball cleanly off the sand, lifted it over the dunes and onto the firm green just inside of Watrous' ball. Watrous, certainly feeling the pressure, three putted once again to Jones' two putt for par. One Scottish writer later called Jones' second stroke on 17 "... the greatest shot in the history of British golf."

Jones parred the last to win his first British Open Championship — the first American amateur to do so. As another British writer commented at the time, "His victory ... was one of the most popular in the history of athletic sports. He not only won the cup with his golf but the heart of the Britishers by his demeanor and character."

Bob returned home to a wholly unexpected welcome in New York and the U.S. Open at Scioto in Columbus, Ohio.

In an amusing moment at the trophy presentation ceremony, Walter Hagen presents a giant niblick to Bob Jones prior to Jones receiving the British Open trophy.

☞ On the deck of the *SS Aquitania* as it steams into New York Harbor, runner-up Al Watrous and Walter Hagen, who tied for third, with the new British Open Champion Bob Jones.

A HERO'S WELCOME

Bob Jones returned home to a hero's welcome: the traditional ticker tape parade up Broadway.

A contingent of some 200 Atlantans greeted him on a chartered boat him at Quarantine, watched him proceed with great fanfare amidst throngs of cheering New Yorkers and stood by as Mayor Walker greeted him on the steps of City Hall.

It was a hero's welcome for the first amateur in 29 years to win the British Open and the very first American amateur to win the British Open.

Mr. and Mrs. Bob Jones on the deck of *The Macon*.

The official New York City reception ship *The Macon* as it leaves Quarantine with Bob Jones aboard for the big parade up Broadway.

ON TO CITY HALL

The big parade proceeded up Broadway in a celebration worthy of a returning hero.

Among those assembled to greet Bob were Major Cohen, the publisher of *The Atlanta Journal* who was representing the Mayor of Atlanta, as well as Bob's parents, grandparents and wife Mary, who had come up to New York to attend the big party for the conquering hero.

Top: Part of the Atlanta contingent in New York. (Note Bob's fraternal grandfather with the high collar at the extreme left of the front row.)

Above: The start of the parade at The Battery.

☞ Assembled dignitaries on the steps of City Hall: (from second from left in the first row) Al Watrous, Walker Cupper Watts Gunn of Atlanta, New York City Mayor Jimmy Walker, Bob Jones, Walter Hagen and Bob's father, Robert T. Jones, Sr.

TWO OPENS IN ONE YEAR

In the first round of the U.S. Open at Scioto in Columbus, Ohio Jones shot a two under 70, just two strokes off the lead. In the second round the strain of the past few weeks took its toll as Jones ballooned to a 79, the highest single round Bob ever shot in an Open tournament.

Included in his score were two penalty strokes — one on the tenth hole when his ball came to rest against a stone wall that was deemed part of a water hazard. The second came when, as he addressed his putt on the fifteenth green, his ball moved an almost imperceptible fraction of an inch. Although no one else had seen it, he promptly called the penalty on himself.

With a 71 in the third round he was now back in the tournament, just three behind the leader Joe Turnesa. On the seventeenth Jones took the lead but Turnesa, playing two groups ahead, birdied the 480-yard 18th to tie. To win Jones would have to match Turnesa's birdie on 18. With a 300-yard drive and a three-quarter three iron to about 16 feet, Bob two putted for his bird to win his second Open Championship of the year and his second U.S. Open.

Bob Jones had become the first man to win both the British and American Open Championships in the same year.

Above: The famed Jones finish.

Bob Jones receives the U.S. Open trophy from USGA President William Fownes.

HOMECOMING!

Atlanta once again welcomed home "the boy wonder of Dixie" with a rousing welcome. Meeting Bob at the train station, Atlanta hoisted Bob on their shoulders and paraded the two Open trophies triumphantly through the streets.

It was quite a homecoming!

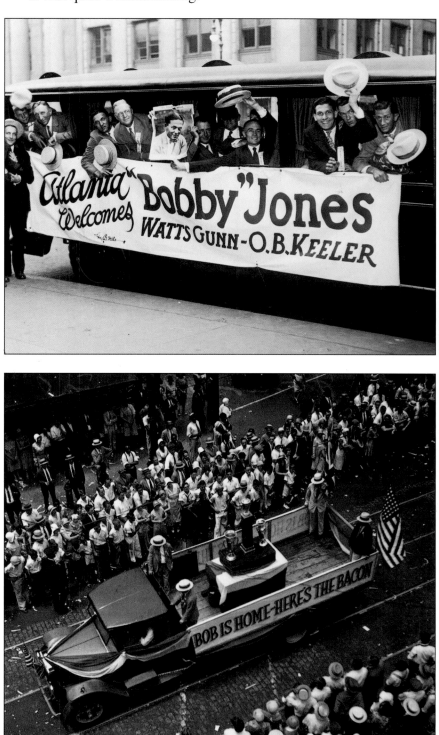

Top: Atlanta excitedly welcomes home Bob Jones, Watts Gunn and O.B. Keeler.

Above: A humorous twist on the adage 'Bring home the bacon'.

Jones' big greeting at the Atlanta train station. Note the two gentlemen leading the procession and holding the U.S. Open and British Open trophies. Holding the British Open trophy is O.B. Keeler.

DEFENDING THE CROWN

Although Bob Jones usually only played golf in Scotland in those years that a Walker Cup was held, he decided to enter the British Open in 1927 not only because he was the defending British Open Champion, but even more so because it was being played on his favorite course, St. Andrews.

In the opening round Bob shot a 68, five under the then par for the course of 73, breaking the course record he had established the day before in qualifying. In the second round, he added a one-under 72 to lead the field by two shots. In the third, he shot his highest round of the Open, a one-over 73, but lengthened his lead to four shots.

Above: Bob Jones in 1927.

⊐ Jones putting on the 13th hole in the third round of play.

"I HAVE ONE REQUEST TO MAKE"

B ob Jones had finished the Open Championship with a second one-under par 72 for a 285 total, the lowest ever for a British Open to that time.

In a gesture that would forever bind him to the Scots, Bob Jones, in accepting the old claret jug emblematic of the British Open Championship, said "I have one request to make and I hope I will be pardoned since I have asked so much from the St. Andrews people. I would take it as a great honor if they would mind the cup for me at St. Andrews."

This act of thoughtfulness and humility forever forged the link between the people of St. Andrews and Bob Jones. One writer described the scene, "It started the second great ovation of the day for Jones. Hats went soaring in the air and fathers hoisted children to their shoulders, to see the young man who is hailed as the greatest exponent of a classic pastime. Stolid old Scots who have not danced a step for decades threw themselves into the Highland fling with the utmost abandon as they danced about the smiling, modest young American."

Bob Jones had successfully defended his British Open Championship at the home of golf.

Above: Bob Jones and his father with the British Open trophy.

 Bob and 'Calamity Jane' after sinking the short putt to gain his second British Open Championship.

ON THE VERGE OF VICTORY

"His second to the last hole was a little cautious and ended in the Valley of Sin. Thence he ran it up dead and as he scaled the bank the crowd stormed up after him and lined the edge of the green, barely restraining themselves."

"He holed his short one and the next instant there was no green visible, only a dark seething mass, in the midst of which was Bobby hoisted on fervent shoulders and holding his putter, "Calamity Jane", at arm's length over his head lest she should be crushed to death."

— Bernard Darwin

☞ Bob Jones, with this short putt, captured the 1927 British Open Chanpionship.

THE YEAR'S FINAL TOURNAMENT

After successfully defending his British Open Championship over the Old Course at St. Andrews, Bob came home to play in his final tournament of the year, the U.S. Amateur at the Minikahda Club in Minneapolis.

As had happened numerous times coming into major championships, Bob was not playing well in the practice rounds. However, after qualifying easily and winning the medal with rounds of 75 and 67 for a 142 total, Jones squeaked by with a 78 in an 18th green victory over Maurice McCarthy, Jr. and won a 3 and 2 victory over Eugene Homans in the second round.

Bob Jones at Minikahda.

◄ Bob Jones hits his second to the long par-five ninth in the final against Chick Evans.

Bob Jones with his good friend Francis Ouimet at the 1927 U.S. Amateur.

☞ Bob Jones is presented the U.S. Amateur trophy by USGA President W.C. Fownes as runner-up Chick Evans looks on.

☜ Chick Evans looks on as Bob Jones putts.

THE THIRD AMATEUR VICTORY

hile the first two rounds were played over 18 holes, the remaining three rounds were played over 36. Jones played extremely well in the remainder of his matches beating Jimmy Johnson 10 and 9 in the quarter finals and then defeated Francis Ouimet in the semifinals 11 and 10.

In the final Bob came up against his old rival Chick Evans. In 1920 Evans had beaten Jones in the Western Open (almost a private reserve for Evans) and Jones had defeated Evans 3 and 2 in the third round of the 1926 U.S. Amateur.

Jones started the 36-hole final strongly with birdies to win the 2nd and 4th holes and pars to win the 3rd and 8th holes. On the par-five 9th — a 512-yard brute with a long uphill second shot to the green where even the biggest hitters normally laid up, Bob hit his second less than two feet from the hole for the first recorded eagle on that hole. With a 31 on the front, Bob was five up on Evans.

The match ended on the 29th hole of the scheduled 36-hole final with Jones winning 8 and 7. Bob Jones had won his third U.S. Amateur in most convincing fashion.

SPECIAL COLLECTIONS DEPARTMENT R.W. WOODRUFF LIBRARY EMORY UNIVERSITY

THE BETTMANN ARCHIVE

THE 1928 U.S. AMATEUR

In the second round of the 1928 Amateur at Brae Burn Country Club near Boston, Bob Jones played one of the most memorable shots of his career. One down on the 11th hole and approximately 200 yards from the green in heavy rough and with his opponent already on the green, Jones hit a towering four-iron over tall trees fifteen feet from the hole, averting a sure loss, as he somehow halved the hole with a birdie four.

Bob went on to defeat reigning British Amateur Champion Philip Perkins in the final, 10 and 9, for his fourth U.S. Amateur title.

Top: Philip Perkins and Bob Jones before the start of the final match.

Above: Bob Jones and the U.S. Amateur trophy.

Left: The third round match went to the 19th hole with Jones defeating Robert Gorton.

ALMOST A DISASTER

The 1929 U.S. Open was scheduled at the Winged Foot Golf Club in Mamaroneck, New York, an A.W. Tillinghast masterpiece, featuring long tree-lined fairways and elevated pear-shaped putting surfaces.

Although the inaugural U.S. Open at Winged Foot was scheduled for the East Course, heavy rains on the eve of the Championship caused a move to the West Course.

Jones shot a 69 in the opening round, his first sub-70 round in the U.S. Open. Interestingly, he went out in 38 strokes - including two double bogeys, but came back in 31, including five consecutive threes to begin the backside, to tie the record for the lowest nine hole score in a U.S. Open and take the first round lead.

Playing in the rain on the afternoon of second day, Jones shot a 75 to fall two behind the leaders. In the morning round of the then traditional double-round final day, Bob shot a fine 71 over the water-laden course to take a lead of three strokes over Gene Sarazen and four over Al Espinosa.

The fourth round saw Jones once again take a 38 on the outward nine, including a triple bogey seven on the eighth hole, the most difficult hole on the course. Espinosa, his sole persuer now, was also having trouble. Jones had a seemingly insurmountable six-shot lead as he reached the 12th hole.

Bob tried to protect his lead by playing safe, as he had so disastrously at Olympia Fields the year before. In doing so, he dissipated his lead over the next few holes, needing three fours over the final three holes to win. He reached the par-5 16th in two, but three putted from twenty feet. He now needed two pars over the remaining two holes just to force a playoff.

He got his par on the 17th.

Large crowds followed Bob Jones on the golf course.

BIRDIE TO WIN,
PAR TO TIE

Jones' drive off the final tee of regulation play was true but his iron shot into the green was pulled into a grassy lie next to a deep bunker below the putting surface on the left hand side of the green.

His pitch left him twelve feet shy of the hole with a tricky side hill breaking putt.

☞ Bob Jones pitches to the 18th green in the final round. From this position on the left side of the green, Jones needed to get up and down to force a playoff.

A TOUCHY TWELVE FOOTER TO TIE

ob Jones needed this last remaining putt to salvage his Open. Not to win, just to tie and force a playoff.

Al Watrous, runner-up to Jones in the 1926 British Open and Jones' playing companion in the final two rounds, described the final sidehill 12-foot putt, "Bob hit a perfect putt that had just the right speed as it hung on the upper edge of the hole for a fraction and then dropped onto the hole."

It has been said that if Bob Jones had missed that curling side hill putt after dissipating such a huge lead, it would have destroyed the hypercritical Jones and his career would have just ended there. Even O.B. Keeler, Jones' confidant and mentor, commented, "I've always believed that the remainder of Bobby's career hung on that putt and that from this, stemmed the Grand Slam of 1930".

But, in one of the heroic finishes in all of golf lore, Bob Jones indeed made the putt with one of his patented putts that died sublimely into the cup to force a 36-hole playoff with Al Espinosa.

The historic 12 foot putt on the 18th green in the final round.

THE PLAYOFF

I n the thirty-six hole playoff that followed on Sunday, Bob Jones completely dominated play by shooting an even par 72 in the morning and a three under 69 in the afternoon to overwhelm Al Espinosa by 23 strokes.

Jones and Espinosa shake hands before the begining of the scheduled playoff.

◁ Jones tees off on the par-3 10th hole as Al Espinosa and USGA President Findley Douglas look on.

THE TROPHY PRESENTATION

As Herb Wind so eloquently summed-up the 1929 Open, "Bob Jones remained the champion of champions."

In winning the 1929 U.S. Open Bob Jones had now extended his streak of winning a major championship to seven years.

Because of the manner in which Jones won the Open at Winged Foot, the West Course became the more celebrated of the two courses. All subsequent Men's Opens played at Winged Foot have been played on the West Course.

JULES ALEXANDER / ATLANTA ATHLETIC CLUB

Top: The golf ball used by Bob Jones in defeating Al Espinosa in the playoff for the 1929 U.S. Open. This is one of the few golf mementos that Jones kept in his office.

Below: Bob Jones with the U.S. Open trophy at Winged Foot.

WORLD WIDE PHOTO

☞ USGA President Findley Douglas presents Bob Jones with his third U.S. Open trophy as Al Espinosa looks on.

THE MEETING

lthough he did not make a public pronouncement of his goal, Bob Jones began the 1930 campaign with the clear-cut objective of winning all four of the major events. The idea first came to him in 1926 when he thought there was a possibility of capturing each of the British and Americans Opens and Amateurs. Although the opportunity presented itself only once every four years — it had to be a Walker Cup year with the British hosting the Matches, this was his big chance at achieving a seemingly impossible goal.

During the winter months Bob played a game that was a cross between badminton and tennis, but played indoors, to keep his weight down. The game was conceived by his movie star friend Doug Fairbanks who had sent him the necessary equipment.

Uncharacteristically Jones entered two early season events, the Savannah Open in February and the Southeastern Open in March. Despite a course record 65 in the third round, Bob finished second in the Savannah Open one stroke behind Horton Smith, his roommate for the week. This was the last golf tournament Bob Jones would ever loose.

In the Southeastern Open at Augusta, Bob completely dominated the field winning by a whopping 13 strokes despite throwing away five strokes on the last three holes. It was here that Jones received a crucial tip from Horton Smith as he learned how to play the short pitch shot, the one possible weak spot in his game. As Bob later acknowledged, "... from Augusta onward during the 1930 season, my pitching was better than it ever was before." His new found proficiency with the pitch shot served him well throughout his quest for the Grand Slam, but especially at the British Open at Hoylake.

So dominating was his performance at Augusta that Bobby Cruickshank spoke most prophetically of Jones, "He's simply too good. He'll go to Britain and win the Amateur and the Open, and then he'll come back over here and win the Open and the Amateur. He is playing too well to be stopped this year."

☞ Four officials of the USGA who attended the executive session at the Hotel Biltmore to set dates for the coming year's championship and otherwise plan the 1930 program. Jimmy Johnson, U.S. Amateur Champion, Findley S. Douglas, USGA President, Bob Jones, U.S. Open Champion, and Jerry Travers.

WALKER CUP CAPTAIN

ob Jones was named captain of the United States Walker Cup team by the Executive Committee of the United States Golf Association for the competition at the Royal St. George's Golf Club in Sandwich on the southeastern coast of England. As captain of the U.S. team, it was his responsibility to name the pairings for the foursomes and to slot the individuals for the singles competition.

For the first team Jones named George Von Elm and George Voigt; for the second he picked Harrison "Jimmy" Johnson and Francis Ouimet; for the third he chose himself and Dr. O.F. Willing; and for the fourth pairing he selected Don Moe, the youngest member of the team, and Roland MacKenzie.

In a gesture wholly consistent with his deferential attitude toward his fellow competitors, Bob named Jimmy Johnson, the reigning U.S. Amateur Champion, to the number one playing position in the singles competition, although Bob's record would certainly have accorded him that distinction.

Above: The American Walker Cup Team at Sandwich. (Back Row; left to right) Roland Mackenzie, Bob Jones, Don Moe, George Voigt; (Front Row) Harrison Johnson, Dr. C.F. Willing, Francis Ouimet, George Von Elm.

Bob Jones and Roger Wethered, captains of the Walker Cup teams.

A ROUT

The 1930 Walker Cup Matches proved to be a rout - only the two Georges, Von Elm and Voigt, lost in the foursomes and Ouimet was the only American to be defeated in the singles. The American side won 10 to 2.

Jones gave an indication of the sterling play to come by playing well in the Walker Cup —he and Doc Willing easily won their alternate shot competition by a score of 8 and 7 and Bob dominated Roger Wethered in their singles match, winning on the 28th hole of the scheduled 36-hole match, 9 and 8.

Above: Large crowds watched the Walker Cup.

R.W. Hartley and Bob Jones walk to the next tee in the four-somes competition at Sandwich.

A RECORD WALKER CUP PERFORMER

Bob Jones compiled one of the very finest Walker Cup records in history. In the five matches Jones played from the inauguration of the competition in 1922 to his last competition in 1930 (he missed only the 1923 matches due to his studies at Harvard), Bob set two records that stand to this day: he won five consecutive singles matches in each of these Walker Cups and his defeat of Phil Perkins in 1928, by a score of 13 and 12, was the widest in Walker Cup history.

Jones lost only one time in his Walker Cup career, losing one down to the British team of Michael Scott and Robert Scott, Jr. in the foursomes competition in the 1924 matches at Garden City Golf Club while paired with William C. Fownes, Jr.

Jones and Wethered congratulate each other at the conclusion of play.

☞ Roger Wethered watches as Bob Jones drives at Sandwich.

"THE MOST IMPORTANT TOURNAMENT OF MY LIFE"

"If I had to select one course upon which to play the match of my life, I should have selected the Old Course."

"I had taken great pains to learn the locations of all the little pot bunkers and felt that I had a complete familiarity with all the devious little slopes and swales which could deflect well-intended shots in such exasperating ways. ...I felt very confident that I should encounter no opponent having an advantage over me on the score of local knowledge."

— Bob Jones

Bob Jones looks over the Swilken Burn at St. Andrews.

☞ Bob Jones was the object of the photographers fancy at the start of the 1930 British Amateur at the Old Course.

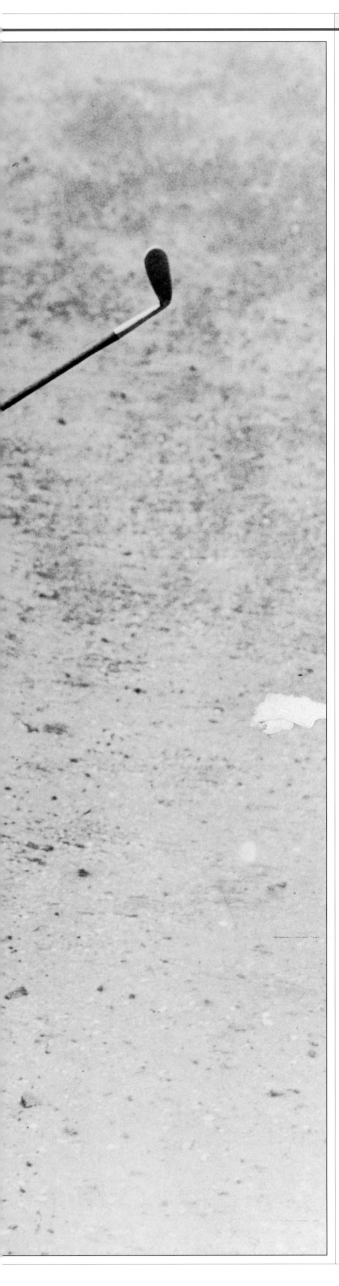

AN EAGLE TWO!

I n the first round Jones played Sid Roper, an ex-coal miner from Nottinghamshire. Expecting a relatively easy match, Bob finally won on the 16th 3 and 2. His eagle two on the 4th hole was one of the most spectacular shots of the tournament: a drive of some 300 yards into Cottage Bunker and a spade mashie of approximately 140 yards that went into the hole.

In the second round he handily defeated Cowan Shankland, 5 and 3.

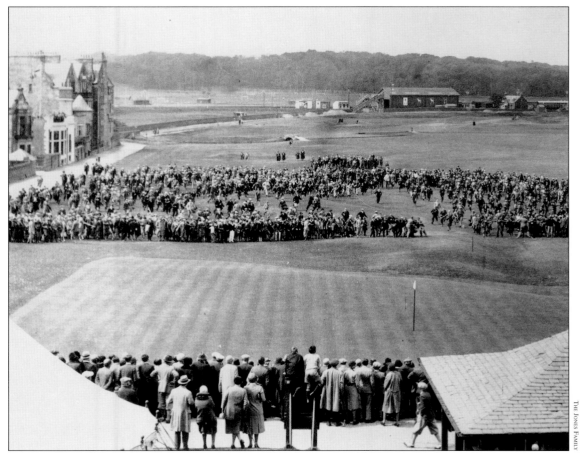

This photograph of Bob playing the 18th hole was taken by his wife Mary from their room in the old Grand Hotel.

Bob played fellow Walker Cup team member Harrison Johnston in the sixth round.

Bob played R. W. Fiddian in the seventh round. The British press somewhat derisively described Fiddian as an artisan golfer.

On the fourth hole Jones' tee shot landed in "Cottage" bunker, approximately 140-yards from the green. He holed the shot for an eagle two.

"IT WAS THE DEVIL OF A MATCH." — Bernard Darwin

"Tolley was one of those players who had a flair for the spectacular ... he played the game, like Hagen, in the grand manner. He was a big, powerful player with an exquisite touch in the short game, and in my opinion the most dangerous man I could possibly meet in an eighteen-hole match at St. Andrews." — Bob Jones

yril Tolley, the defending British Amateur Champion, met Jones in the fourth round. The match was eagerly anticipated and virtually the entire population of St. Andrews turned out to watch. And they were not disappointed by any stretch of the imagination.

Tolley's only apparent mistake for 18 holes was a full-fledged top off the first tee. Never separated by more than one hole, the match was all even on the famed 17th—the Road Hole—the turning point of several of Jones's matches during the Amateur. Neither player took the short way off the tee by driving over Aucherlonie's drying sheds so as to cut the dog leg and leave a shorter shot into the green. Tolley played safely to the left side of the fairway and Jones played even further left.

Cyril then played his second just short of the green, leaving a short pitch shot to the somewhat elevated green. Bob decided to go for the green in two with a cut spoon - a faded two wood by today's reckoning, but his shot just cleared the Road Bunker, bounded through the green and was headed for the Road and sure oblivion when, luckily, his ball hit a spectator on the back fringe of the green. Both players made their fours.

Both halved the home hole with pars. Moving onto the first extra hole, both drove well, but Tolley's second was off line and, after a somewhat indifferent shot into the green, Bob's putt laid Tolley a stymie which he failed to negotiate. As Bernard Darwin later wrote, "It was the devil of a match."

"It was the kind of match in which each player plays himself so completely out that at the end the only feeling to which he is sensitive is one of utter exhaustion." — Bob Jones

Top: Tolley and Jones after their epic match.
Above: Jones drives from the tee

☞ Jones searches for his ball in his match against Tolley.

"... ON HIS WAY TO THE GRAND SLAM."

"We had a tremendous gallery—people lined from tee to green on every hole and so deep that most of them couldn't see. It was my honor on the par-five 14th hole, and I had been hitting the ball so straight that going out of bounds never entered my mind. I tried to cut a corner, as I had been doing, but the ball drifted like a balloon in the wind and blew over the fence. I was out of bounds by about a foot.

Jones seemed to perk up here. He played his drive much safer to the left and won the hole with a par.

On the par-four 15th we both were about two feet from the hole in three, but I was away by an inch. I putted and missed, and everybody, myself included, thought he would make his little putt and square the match. But he missed, and I was still one up.

A series of three pot bunkers called the Principal's Nose sits left center of the 16th fairway. By then I had played the course a few times in practice and in seven rounds of Championship, and I had never given those bunkers a thought. Jones drove down the left side of the fairway, and then I hit my drive into the Principal's Nose. He won the hole with a par 4 and we were even with two hole to play.

The 17th is 467 yards long, and I was on the front edge in two with a drive and a one-iron. Bob was short and chipped about 12 feet from the hole, leaving himself a curling, side-hill putt.

I almost made my putt, left it on the lip, and he had to make this seemingly impossible putt or else I was going to be one up with one to play.

I didn't think he would make it and I don't think anybody in the gallery thought he would make it. He stood over the ball a little longer than usual and stroked it in the middle of the hole: It was never in doubt. We halved the hole in fours.

We both drove in the fairway on the 18th and I was away. The approach called for a club a little longer than the spade mashie I used (about an eight-iron) but the next club in my bag was a mashie (about a five-iron).

I hit what I thought was a perfect shot, but it hit the slope leading to the upper level of the two-level green and rolled back into the Valley of Sin, the bottom part of the green, and about 80 feet from the hole. Bob's second shot was about 15 feet from the hole.

I hit a good putt from 80 feet, about two feet from the hole. Bobby lipped the cup for his birdie and I had to make mine to send the match into extra holes.

I was a little shaky; I didn't want to stand over the ball. I thought the more I studied it the more nervous I would be. I gave it a quick look, hit what I thought was a good putt, but it lipped the cup and stayed out. Bob was in the final and on his way to the Grand Slam."

— *George Voight*

All square on the 18th tee, Bob Jones defeated George Voight on the last green to move into the final.

Voight intently watches Jones drive on the 14th hole.

THE FINAL MATCH

E ntering the final match of the 1930 British Amateur against Englishman Roger Wethered, Bob Jones was at the top of his game. He had made it through seven grueling 18-hole matches and he was finally within striking distance of his goal of winning the one major championship that had eluded him.

Playing a 36-hole match was his strength: he felt that he need not be afraid of someone getting hot over a short 18-hole match; he could steadily apply pressure by playing against "Old Man Par" and hope his opponent would crack. He simply felt he needed the room of an 36-hole match to maneuver.

Bob Jones was confident and he was ready.

Above: Jones plays his way out of trouble.

Right: Wethered congratulates Jones after their final round match in the 1930 British Amateur.

Crowds escorting Bobby Jones at St. Andrews during the final round of the British Amateur Championship.

ONLY 36 HOLES TO GO

Although Bob played the front nine in one under par, the match was all even. He finally went one up on the 10th, halfed the 11th and 12th, but then Bob won the next four holes to go five up at the luncheon break. After the first nine holes of the second 18, he was still five up. For the second time he won the 10th to go six up and closed Wethered out on the 13th to win his one and only British Amateur Championship.

 Bob Jones is escorted by policemen through the friendly crowd that mobbed him after the finish of the 1930 British Amateur at St. Andrews.

The Times

No. 45,528   LATE LONDON EDITION   LONDON, MONDAY, JUNE 2, 1930   Price 2d.

Sporting News

GOLF

R.T. JONES AMATEUR CHAMPION

THE PERFECT GOLFER

(FROM OUR GOLF CORRESPONDENT)

ST. ANDREWS, May 31

R. T. Jones beat R. H. Wethered by seven up and six to play in the final of the Amateur Championship over the Old Course to-day. He has now caught up Alexander the Great and has no more Championships to win. He played just as we have always been told he did in a 36-hole match, unhasting, unrelenting, playing not so much against a flesh-and-blood enemy as against the perfect score for the course. In the first round there was never a ghost of a flaw. In the afternoon he seemed for one brief moment to be growing unsettled and then came back to that rhythmic and unbroken stride under which he has trampled the whole world of golf like some inevitable juggernaut. It was so magnificent that it hardly seemed to be golf; it was rather the progress of a mechanical creature which is wound up and goes on clicking round the course for ever and ever.

The match was much more exciting than the final result would indicate, and Wethered made a fine fight of it against overwhelming odds. He did hit a few crooked drives in the morning, but generally speaking his wooden club play was good. It would be unfair to say he lost the match by driving. It is truer to say, in Jack White's words, that "This man Jones is teaching us that matches can be won by driving." Wethered's iron play; as superb and unfaltering, and his approach putts were well struck and not blessed with much luck. He did fail to some extent in the shorter putts. All the week he had been holing the middle length and short putts beautifully, but to-day he seemed to be moving his body just a fraction too soon and not, as he usually does, after the ball is on its way. He had several good chances on the green which he did not hole. If he could have taken them, he might have made a much closer thing of it, but it is hardly conceivable that he ever could have won.

AN EXCITING START

The first round began by sending agreeable shivers of excitement down the spine, for after Wethered had played a lovely second to within four yards or so of the hole Jones missed his pitch so completely that the ball stopped short of the Burn. He played an excellent third and holed his putt; Wethered just failed to get his 3, and the hole was halved. The luck evened itself at the second, where Wethered bombarded the wall with a fierce hook and the ball came back on to grass. He played a fine second and halved in four with Jones, who had played the hole like a plaster saint. From this point it would be a waste of words to describe Jones's play in minute detail, since it never varied; a vast straight drive down the course, a good second with some iron club, and then a putt which was generally stone dead and seldom more than 4ft. away. He had settled down to his old, familiar gait in long matches, which has broken so many opponents. "Keep on shooting par at them and they'll all crack" is his motto on these occasions and he acted up to it so fully that when he had a shortish putt to beat par he seemed positively averse from holing it.

A sundial counts only the sunny hours; I will do the converse and only record the few shots, all putts, which Jones missed. Wethered offers a wider field for description. He took three putts at the third to be one down, and then played a truly magnificent approach to the fourth giving him a chance of a 3, which he could not quite take. To the Heathery Hole he cut his drive away into the heather, whence he played the most divine of pitch-and-run shots over the hill and through the hollow to lie stone dead. That made the match square again and after two good halves Jones did something worthy of record. At the ninth Wethered hit the most colossal of hooks from the tee, but recovered and got his 4. Jones had a 4ft. or 5ft. putt to win in three and missed it, so the match was still all square with both players out in 35—very fine figures, but obtained more easily by one than the other.

Wethered took three putts at the 10th and that was one down. He seemed likely to square at the 11th until Jones holed a horrid, sidling putt of 6 ft. I suppose he holed it because he had it to keep even with the great god par and not to beat him. At the 13th he had quite a short one for a 3, but that would have been one better than par, and therefore he missed it. So Jones was still only one up and Wethered was playing his irons like a hero and hanging on nobly. But the strain had to tell soon, and now the inevitable happened. Wethered recovered from a sliced second at the Hole o' Cross, but failed at the final putt; two down. He recovered splendidly from the edge of Hell bunker at the Long Hole, but the inexorable Jones obviously regarded this as a par 4 and holed a 10ft. putt to win it accordingly. At the 15th Wethered took three putts after his long putt looked as if it must drop, and at the Corner of the Dyke he went out of bounds. That was five up to Jones, and the interest shifted momentarily from the match to the subsidiary question whether Jones could get round St. Andrews without a single 5. Wethered played the odd to the 17th and rightly took every risk. The ball pitched just to the right of the Road bunker, hard against the bank, gave one hop, and lay four yards from the pin. Jones also went straight at it, and his ball ended in the bunker under the green. The crowd was carefully cleared away from the back to give him a chance of going from the bunker into the road. The great man smiled indulgently at the stewards and, playing a really miraculous shot, half gentle and half explosive, laid the ball 4ft. from the pin and then—a sad anti-climax—he missed the putt and had that one black blot of a 5 after all. The home hole was halved in four, and Wethered finished four down. Jones had taken one 5, two 3's, and 15 4's. I do not think I ever saw golf so well played in all my life. The scores were:

JONES

OUT:	4, 4, 4, 4, 4, 4, 4, 3, 4 35
HOME:	4, 3, 4, 4, 4, 4, 4, 5, 4 36

71

WETHERED

OUT:	4, 4, 5, 4, 4, 3, 4, 3, 4 35
HOME:	5, 3, 4, 5, 5, 5, 6, 4, 4 41

76

THE SECOND ROUND

After luncheon there was a prodigious crowd, but it was good-tempered and docile and well shepherded by an army of stewards, including one Amazon with a red flag and a periscope. The start was a dramatic one, and looked for a little while as if it might turn the tide in Wethered's favour. Both played splendid pitches to the first hole, Jones to within 7ft. and Wethered to within 6ft. Jones tried for his 3 and ran 2ft. past. Wethered missed also, but laid a dead stymie which Jones failed to loft. So in place of a likely half in three the hole had been won in four against five and one was lopped off the lead. At the second hole Wethered went right down the course and Jones hit a really wild hook. The ball seemed bound for perdition under the wall if not through the gate, but was stopped, I think, by the crowd. At any rate it finished lying tolerably clean on the road, and thence Jones played a heroic pitch over all the bunkers and on to the bank behind the green. Thence he very nearly holed his putt and laid Wethered, who was eight or nine yards away, a dead stymie. Wethered had to get past the hole; he played the shot well, lay apparently dead, and then, amid groans of horror, missed his short putt. It certainly was the very cruelest tit for tat for the first hole. There had been hopes of down to two up; now it was four up again and all real hope was gone. The next three hole was halved, Wethered missing a not very long putt at the fourth; and every hole halved was now almost a hole gained for the leader. At the sixth Wethered holed a 12-yard putt for 3, amid frantic demonstrations, but he tried to do the same thing at the seventh, ran past and was duly laid a hopeless stymie. That really was the end. He lost the eighth, where he was bunkered. Jones drove on to the edge of the 10th green and got his 3 to be six up. Wethered made a gallant effort for a 2 at the 11th and failed by an inch. It was the last dying kick, for he took 5 to the 12th, and Bobby ended with yet one more 4, his twenty-second 4 out of 40 holes played.

The winner was at once swallowed up in a cheering mob and ultimately got home by the road with four stalwart constables as an escort. He can never come too often or win too often for a St. Andrews crowd. The scores were:

JONES

OUT:	5, 4, 4, 5, 4, 4, 4, 3, 4 37
HOME:	3, 3, 4

WETHERED

OUT:	4, 5, 4, 5, 4, 3, 5, 4, 4 38
HOME:	4, 3, 5

☞ Col. Skene of the Royal and Ancient presents the 1930 British Amateur trophy to Bob Jones.

HOYLAKE

After Bob Jones' stirring victory in the British Amateur at St. Andrews, he and Mary went to Paris for a break before the British Open began at the Royal Liverpool Golf Club in Hoylake, England. While in France, he played an exhibition match against several leading French golfers and toured the area around the French capital. Well rested, he returned to England and remarked that he was looking forward to eating some cold English mutton after all of the heavy French food.

Undoubtedly content with his victory in the British Amateur, the one major championship he had not won, Bob's game had slipped into a malaise on the eve of the British Open. The strongest aspects of his game — driving and putting — were ragged and he just did not seem to have that old fire. (This pattern of lacksidasical play on the eve of a major championship had been a somewhat recurring one throughout Jones' career.) Nevertheless, he qualified easily with a two round total of 150, although this was nine strokes behind the medalist Archie Compston.

In the first round Bob buckled down and shot a sharp two-under par 70 and tied with MacDonald Smith and Henry Cotton for the first round lead. In the second round, he added an even-par 72, for a one stroke lead.

☞ Bob Jones drives from the eighth tee in the first round of play of the British Open at Hoylake.

Inset: Bob Jones, recently crowned British Amateur Champion, with Jimmy Johnston, the 1929 U.S. Amateur Champion, on the St. Germain course near Paris as they played an exhibition with M. Dellamagne, the French Professional Champion, and M. Vagliane, the French Amateur Champion.

THE THIRD ROUND

Jones struggled in the third round as he shot a two-over par 74. As Bob played the first four holes of the third round in two-over par, Archie Compston, playing magnificently, played them in three under par, effectively gaining five whole strokes in the course of just four holes.

Settling down, Bob played the next nine holes in two-under. Faced with the grueling final five holes at Hoylake, among the most difficult finishing holes in all of golf, Jones finished with four fives and one four for a two-over total of 74 for the third round. Compston, playing about a half an hour behind Jones, carded a superb 68 to grab the lead.

Jones putts on the 7th green in the first round.

THE FINAL ROUND

J ust as Compston was triumphantly completing his third round on the 18th green, Bob was teeing off for his final round in the double round final day. Jones got his par four on the first, but on the relatively short 369-yard par four 2nd hole Bob sliced his drive to the right. Incredibly, his ball hit a steward squarly on the head — reports of the incident claim he was not hurt — and it traveled about 40 yards forward into a bunker on the 14th hole. With a clean lie, Bob lofted his sand shot of 140 yards onto the second green some twenty feet from the pin and holed the putt for a birdie three. What looked like a sure five or worse, had turned into a three!

At about this same time, Compston, playing his fourth shot at the first hole — a simple putt of about a foot and a half for par — somehow missed. And with it, all of the bravado and confidence of the morning's round 68 seemed to dissipate, as he finished with a dissappointing final round of 82.

Not playing easily, Jones fought his way home to a final round 75, edging Leo Diegel and Mac Smith. As Herb Wind commented, "At Hoylake Bobby had won through patience and guts and philosophy and instinct".

In doing so he won his third British Open in a row and the third in four tries.

Bob Jones off the tee at Hoylake.

Jones comes out of the sand.

The Times

No. 45,545   LONDON, SATURDAY, JUNE 21, 1930   Price 4d.

Sporting News

GOLF

R.T. JONES'S DOUBLE

STIRRING FINISH AT HOYLAKE

(FROM OUR GOLF CORRESPONDENT)
HOYLAKE, June 20

Forty years ago Mr. John Ball won the Amateur and the Open Championship in the same year. Now Bobby Jones has equalled that record, an, as far as I know, he has no more records to equal or worlds to conquer. He can retire with a quiet mind, and well he may, for I do not think that anyone ever suffered more tortures in winning a championship than he did in winning this one.

It was a triumph of courage and of putting. Up to the green he was not playing with confidence. Sometimes he was almost ragged, but his glorious touch on the greens never left him, and he never gave in, though once in the last round he came, as I fancy, within measurable distance of doing so. Everybody who was really in the hunt had his bad moments and wilted a little, Jones like the rest, but his finish, when he knew that every stroke was of supreme importance, was magnificent, and if he has played better he has never played more bravely.

And now to begin at the beginning of a long and harrowing day. The morning's golf began just after 8 o'clock, when Horton Smith started in grey, still weather with a few drops of rain. He had a great chance of getting his blow in first and frightening every one else, but he did not take it. A 6 at the first hole was the herald of an unworthy round. He took 40 to the turn and 38 home. Though not bad in itself, it was not good enough to mend matters; 223 was bound to throw him a number, of valuable strokes behind.

Next came the man who appeared the brightest British hope, Robson, and there was no single Englishman on the course who would not have rejoiced to see him win. This round was a tragic record of missed putts; 4, 5, 5, for the first three holes seemed harmless enough when he played a beauty to the Cop and gave himself a putt for 2. Alas! he managed to take 4 and his putting confidence was badly shaken. Every stroke up to the pin was beautifully struck, but the short ones would not drop, and what should have

been 36 to the turn became 39. At the 10th he did hole a fine putt for 3, and we hoped that this marked the turning of the tide, but it was not to be. He missed another four-footer at the 11th, trying all to plainly to steer the ball in to the hole instead of hitting it there. Who is there who does not know the horrid feeling? Another putt went astray at the 12th, and though he stuck to it manfully, 78 is not good enough.

JONES'S ROUND

Now for Bobby Jones, who once again showed that, if he gets frightened of a certain hole or series of holes, he is as human as any of us. He was lucky at the first hole, missing the Sandy Ditch by a fraction of an inch. A grand second got him a 4 and now we thought the wicked magician's spell was broken and he would go ahead like a house on fire. But not a bit of it. A long drive at the second was caught in the hay, his second shot was bunkered, and he did well to get a 5. Worse was to come. One drive hooked out of bounds, and then, after a good rub, a brassey shot pushed far out into the rough. That meant a 6, and though, to be sure, he had lost nothing to either Horton Smith or Robson, he had yet hung the old millstone round his neck. Still, once more he settled down to play like an angel to the turn. Thirty-seven was as good as he could hope for, and he made things better still by holing a beauty for a 3 on the sloping 10th green; 3, 4, 3, was the proper score for the next three holes, and he got it, and that without an effort. So in the course of 10 holes 3 over 4's had miraculously become 2 under 4's and the stage seemed set for a 70 or a 71. Even Jones, however, can take 5's at those fierce long holes that make the end of Hoylake so formidable, and he took four 5's in a row. Three of them were venial enough, but the three putts on the Royal Green were unworthy of the most beautiful putter in the world. A 4 at the last gave him 74, and an average of 4's for the three rounds.

A STRONG ATTACK

Goodness knows that this was good enough , but still it laid him open to attach, and, in fact, a tremendous attack was developing some five holes behind him. Compston's progress was punctuated by bursts of cheering, which could be heard all over the links. He began 4, 3, 4, and then holed a 10-yard putt for a 2 at the Cop. At this point he had regained the whole of the

five strokes by which Jones had led him after two rounds. A set-back followed when he hooked his drive into a bad place at the fifth. However, he played a sensible man's part, tried for nothing too ambitious and might well have got a 5. In fact, he took 6, and had lost a couple of strokes to the leader. Now was the crucial moment, and Compston never wavered, but went on 4, 3, 4, 4, for 34 to the turn. That was good enough, but better was to come. It seemed impossible that he could pick up any more strokes from Jones in the first four holes homeward, but he did. Jones had done 3, 3, 4, 3; Compston did 3, 3, 3, 2, and at every fresh exploit a wild yell of defiance or exultation rent the air. When the rumour came back to the Club House that he was 7 under 4's nobody would believe it, but for once it was true, and a 67 or a 66 seemed possible. Compston has a fine nerve and an invincible courage but even he must have felt rather light-headed, and doubted whether he was on his head or his heels. It would have been astounding if he had not let a stroke or two slip, and in fact he took a bad and quite unnecessary 6 at the Dun, playing a weak run up and missing a tiny putt. He steadied himself, however, and ended with two 5's for his 68. What a wonderful score when it simply had to be done, and when it had two 6's in it! He broke the record by two shots and led Jones by one. Here are his figures:

OUT:	4, 3, 4, 2, 6, 4, 3, 4, 4	34
HOME:	3, 3, 3, 2, 5, 4, 6, 4, 4	34

Even so it was not certain that he would lead, for Diegel, close behind him, was going almost as splendidly round, as Compston had done. He reached the turn one better in 33 and went on with 3, 3, 5, 3. After being well placed near the green in 2, he mysteriously managed take a 6. Diegel is the most "temperamental" of all golfers, but he has plenty of pluck. He returned to the attack, ended steadily in 5, 4, 4, and with a 71 finished two behind Jones and three behind Compston.

Barnes, Boyer, and D. K. Moe played fine rounds, and the first two at any rate had a distinct chance, but still it was only the three leaders that really seemed to count, and Jones was the first of them to go out. If only he could for once start well, he was just where he like to be, not actually leading, but in such a position as to come away in the last round. He did start with a 4 at first and then an amazing 3 at the second. His

ball pitched on the head of a steward, and a very resilient head he must have, for the ball bounded miles away into a bunker that is meant to catch people going to the Field hole. He played a grand shot out right on to the green, and holed a five-yard putt. Now he was off, and everything was lovely till he came to the eighth, where he had the most ridiculous and tragical of all 7's. Two great wooden club shots left him a bare 40 yards from the pin. It seemed as if a 12 Handicap player with a croquet mallet could get a 5. Jones was short with his run up, played another weak one and played it rather quickly, went for his putt, missed that, and then missed the tiny one back. It seemed that this loss of an iron self-control, for just one minute had thrown away the Championship, but now we were to see the way to face misfortune. He was out in 38, and did not begin too well home, for he had 4's at both short holes, but he buckled to at the long holes, and finished 4, 5, 4, 4. It was a great effort, and he had to play one great shot, a niblick shot, at the Dun, laid stiff stone dead. The 4 at the Royal was not an easy one, but his 2 nearly had a 3 at the Home Hole. And now we knew to some extent where we were.

Compston started with a crowd of high hopes, but those hopes were soon cruelly dissipated. he began by missing a shortish putt for a 4, and perhaps that began the rot. At any rate it was a terrible rot. One hooked shot followed another and there was a long and gloomy row of 5's. The story is too sad to tell at length, even if it were worth it, and he ended in 82, a pathetic come-down after his heroic work of the morning.

Now Diegel remained, and he was making a great fight of it. Going out he was not good enough, but he holed a great putt for a 3 at the 12th, squirming with agitation as the ball fell in. He had another 3 at the 13th, and now we knew that he wanted one 5 and four 4's to tie. The 5 came at the Field, but he holed a noble putt for his 4 at the Lake, and still he tried. The Dun saw the end. He was bunkered off the tee and took three putts. That was 6. Par 3's to tie was beyond him or anyone else, and he finished in 75, two strokes behind Jones.

All seemed over when there came in great stories of Macdonald Smith, who had finished six strokes behind Jones in the morning. He made a superb effort: went out in 34 and like Diegel, wanted two 3's to tie. Like Diegel, he took two 4's and as his second shot ran past the 18th flag Jones was safe at last.

☞ Bob Jones receives the British Open trophy from the Captain of the Hoylake Golf Club.

THE SECOND TICKER TAPE PARADE

New York once again prepared a big welcome home celebration for America's returning hero — a big ticker tape parade up Broadway and a reception at City Hall.

In 1926 Bob had become the first American amateur to win the British Open and New York rolled out the red carpet for Bob with his first big parade.

Now he had won both the British Amateur *and* the British Open in the same year. And New York feted him with its second ticker tape parade.

Bob arrives in Manhattan for the start of the parade.

Bob Jones waves from the deck of the Mandalay with wife Mary, mother Clara and his father.

A BLIZZARD OF CONFETTI

he procession up Broadway from the Battery was electric. Bob and Mary Jones basked in the well wishes of New York as Pathe News filmed the event for screening in movie theaters across the country and around the world.

The ead car proceeds up Broadway.

1 A slightly embarassed Bob Jones acknowledges the cheers.

CITY HALL RECEPTION

fter the parade reached City Hall, Mayor Jimmy Walker once again welcomed Bob back home to the cheers of New Yorkers.

Bob Jones is the only person ever accorded two ticker tape parades up Broadway.

THE BETTMANN ARCHIVE

USGA

Top: Mayor Walker greets Bob Jones at City Hall.

Above: Mayor Walker commented, "Here I am, the worst golfer in the world introducing the best golfer in the world."

☞ The big parade proceeds up Broadway.

HIGH HEAT AND HUMIDITY

T he weather in the first round was the big story as the thermometer soared to over 100 degrees and the high humidity aggravated the situation. In fact, the uncomfortable conditions were so bad that Cyril Tolley, a large bear of a man and perhaps Britain's finest player, collapsed from the sweltering heat; Bob Jones had to have his tie cut off after his round, because it was so thoroughly soaked with perspiration that it could not be loosened.

However, given his hiatus from golf after the long sea journey home and the big celebration in New York combined with the difficult weather, Bob somehow still managed a one-under-par 71. This left him only one stroke behind the first round co-leaders Tommy Armour and Macdonald Smith.

Above: Jock Hutchinson and Bob Jones as they started the first round of play at the U.S. Open at Interlachen.

Jones drives from the ninth tee in the opening round at Interlachen.

THE "LILY PAD" SHOT

One under par heading into the 485-yard par-5 ninth hole, Jones pushed his tee shot far to the right. Electing to go for the green in two, Bob hit the most bizarre shot of the tournament and one of the luckiest of his career.

Just as he was in the middle of his backswing he noticed two small girls starting to run across the fairway ahead of him. He reacted by half-topping his shot, sending it on a line towards the pond that fronted the green. Just then Providence - or perhaps a lily pad, intervened and the ball skipped across the surface of the pond as if it were a flat stone thrown by a child.

The ball ended up on the green side of the lake only a short pitch away. Bob pitched close and made the putt for a birdie four.

He ended the round with a 73 for a two-day total of even par 144 and tied with Harry Cooper and Charles Lacey for second place, two strokes behind second round leader Horton Smith, going into the final day's traditional double round. Just off the lead were former U.S. Open Champions Johnny Farrell (1928), Tommy Armour (1927) and Walter Hagen (1914 and 1919). It was anyone's tournament.

Although the press reported it as a lily pad, Jones later said no lily pad was involved.

THE FINAL TWO ROUNDS

B ob Jones felt he was in a good position starting the final day of play just two strokes off the lead. He felt he did not have a lead to protect and he could go out and play his game.

Jones played a superlative front nine in the third round, a three under par 33 with birdies at the 4th, 6th and 7th holes. With birdies on the 11th, 12th and 16th, Bob needed to simply par the last two holes for a record 66. Understandably, at this point he felt he was playing as well as he ever had in a major championship — swinging smoothly and comfortably and putting flawlessly. The record was not to be, as he bogied each of the last two holes for a 68, but he was five shots clear of Harry Cooper in second place after three full rounds.

The fourth and final round was a roller coaster of scoring, especially on the four par-three holes. Jones double bogied the 180-yard par-three 3rd hole and then birdied the par-four 4th; although he parred the par-three 5th, he double bogied the 192-yard par-three 13th, but birdied the next two holes, both par-fours; and he then proceeded to make his third double bogey of the afternoon on a par three hole with a five on the 262-yard par-three 17th, after a ruling by USGA referee Prescott Bush.

Coming to the 18th hole and leading by a single stroke, Jones somewhat tentatively placed his second shot on the front of the green, a good 40 feet from the pin. In a spectacular finish to a very up and down round, he made the putt for a final round of 75. Although he had to wait out a late charge by Mac Smith, Bob Jones had won his fourth U.S. Open with a 287 total, his personal best in the national championship.

(Interestingly, the 262-yard par-three 17th hole at Interlachen was the longest par-three hole in U.S. Open history. Jones struggled with the hole throughout the Championship - although he parred it in the first round, he bogied it in the second and third rounds to go along with his double bogey in the final round.)

"As I stepped up to the putt, I was quivering in every muscle. I confess that my most optimistic expectation was to get the thing dead. It is impossible to describe the sensation I felt when I saw my ball take a small break five or six feet from the cup, so I knew it was in."

—Bob Jones

With this birdie four Bob had to wait an hour until Mac Smith, his closest pursuer, came to the 18th needing a two on the par four hole to tie. Smith parred the hole and finished two strokes back. This putt had won the Open for Jones.

AUGUST 1930

*F*OUNDED *November, 1908, and pub-lished monthly. Devoted to the interests of golf and golfers, and the legitimate promo-tion of the game. Independent in its policies and not affiliated with any golf organization.*

*T*HE *aim of this publication is to aid in the development of golf and at the same time to help cultivate in devotees of the game a spirit of good sportsmanship and fair play for which golfers have long been noted.*

Jones Writes More History

Has Now Won a National Title For Eight Years in Succession

By O. B. Keeler

I CAME away from Interlachen with a pro-nounced hunch that it was Bobby Jones' last start in a National Open golf championship, but this is by no means committing Mr. Jones to anything. I know that Bobby's father would be just as pleased, if Bobby stayed out of the big show from now on, and I am even more certain his mother would be pleased, but Bobby—and very properly—declines to say anything about it.

"If I said anything I might have to change my mind," said Bobby a few minutes after it was definitely established that he had won the United States Open Title for the fourth time.

This, by the way, recalls a little conversa-tion we had some five years ago. Just after Bobby had won the National Amateur Championship at Oakmont, Bobby confessed at the time to an ambition, after extracting a promise that I would never write anything about it unless it should happen to be realized.

"Which is not at all likely," said Bobby. This was the ambition admitted by Bobby in 1925 when he had won the United States Open once and the Amateur twice:

"I'd like to be national champion of the United States six years in succession," said Bobby, "Either Open or Amateur. Then I could feel that I had left a sort of dent in the game. You might say it would be some kind of a record, but I don't suppose there is enough chance of it to lose any sleep worrying about it."

I don't know if Bobby has lost any sleep worrying about the record he was compiling year by year and tournament by tournament, but I do know that when he finished at Interlachen he was National Champion of the United States for the eighth year in succession which is two years more than his pet ambition called for back in 1925. He has won four Open championships and four Amateur championships in the last eight years and never both in the same year; his remaining chance to equal somebody else's record is this year, for Chick Evans did this in 1916 at Minikahda and Merion.

Along with the eight American titles, Bobby has captured three British Opens and one British Amateur, a round dozen major championships in all, which puts him one title ahead of Walter Hagen, who has won four British Opens, two United States Opens, and five national professional championships.

Somehow I think seven National Open cham-pionships is enough. Bobby should go pecking away at the Amateur championships in this coun-try and in Britain, if and when he is sent over with our Walker Cup outfit, and I expect to pick up a couple more of these pretty titles before he hangs up his clubs. I do not think he needs to add any-thing more to his record in the Open champi-onships. He may live to be a very old man, but he will never live to see anyone else match his record of the last eight years in the United States Open, four first places and three second places, two of them after a tie and a playoff.

History at Hoylake repeated itself with a curious exactness at Interlachen. In the British Open championship, Bobby led off with a round of 70 and so did MacDonald Smith. At Interlachen, Jones started with a 71 and Mac with a 71. Jones went ahead in the second round at Hoylake, and in the second round at Interlachen, Jones gained a stroke more in the third round at Hoylake and a lot of strokes, six to be exact, in the third round at Interlachen. At Hoylake Jones led Smith by six strokes as the final round began and at Interlachen Bobby had a margin of seven strokes on the silent Scot in the same spot, and at Hoylake and also at Interlachen Bobby got around with a brilliant, but very patchy score of 75, while Mac Smith, playing like a machine, scored a 71 at Hoylake and a 70 at Interlachen to gain four strokes in the British event and five in the American, and finish two strokes back of Jones in each.

Adding to the coincidence, Horton Smith finished five strokes back of Jones and three strokes back of Mac Smith in both the Hoylake and the Interlachen campaigns.

Golf indubitably is the most uncertain of games, and yet in the face of this singularly accurate reproduction in two great champi-onships played in a space of twenty-four days

on courses four thousand miles apart, it is stu-pid to assert that there can be no such thing as playing form. These three great golfers finished these two tournaments in precisely the same positions, all three being four strokes better at Interlachen than at Hoylake, which probably is about the difference in the two courses.

I think the Interlachen course is a bit soft in the first nine, and the number of two-shot holes that a big hitter can reach with a drive and pitch naturally conduces to fast scoring at times. But the layout stood up surprisingly well under the attack of the greatest aggregation of scoring machines that ever entered a golf tournament.

Willie Kidd, the distinguished professional at Interlachen, had the course in the best possible condition, and the tournament organization was remarkable in its completeness and effective-ness. Herbert Ramsay, Bob Curring, Findlay Douglas, and other executives of the United States Golf Association all were at some pains to compliment the Interlachen organization in the highest terms, and I cannot recall a more delight-ful group to work with than John Barton, presi-dent of the club, Charles Van Nest, chairman of the tournament committee, John McNutt, George Labatt, John Burgess and others, who had charge of the multitudinous details of running a great championship. The enormous galleries were handled with exemplary precision and I do not recall any galleries that behaved better.

The newspaper men were accorded every possible convenience for covering the champi-onship and, in the matter of entertainment, Interlachen provided a fine replica of the memorable championship at Minikahda three years ago. The Minikahda club, indeed, through Bert Strong and others gave the visit-ing newspapermen a great dinner party the Wednesday evening before the tournament began, and the Interlachen club gave them another on Friday evening. Courtesy and hos-pitality and real friendship have marked the relations of the golf writers and the clubs in the two great championships played in Minneapolis in the last three years.

☞ Findley Douglas presents the 1930 U.S. Open trophy to Bob Jones.

MERION

"I know no American course could be more to my liking than Merion"
— Bob Jones

And so Bob Jones had back come to the Merion Cricket Club outside of Philadelphia to complete one of the greatest feats ever accomplished in all of sport.

Bob Jones had come full circle — from the time he entered his first national championship at Merion as a brash club-throwing 14-year old in 1916, to the site of his first National Amateur victory at Merion in 1924 and now back to Merion for what was to be his last attempt at a national title and the concluding trick of his Grand Slam.

Jones proceeded to win the medal in the qualifying round with a record setting 69-73—142.

🖙 Since the fairways were not roped in 1930 as they are in major championships today, Jones had to be ushered around the course with flagmen.

🖙 Bob walks down the fairway at the outset of the U.S. Amateur. With Jones are his caddy, Howard Rexford (far left), and O.B. Keeler (on Jones' right).

🖙 America was interested in Jones and the press photographers were certainly on hand to chronicle the great event.

THE DREADED 18-HOLE MATCHES

I n the first round Bob met Sandy Sommerville, the Canadian Amateur Champion and a fine player with a compact and functional swing. The match proved to be the most difficult of the Amateur for Jones.

One up through six holes, both players hit good drives on the seventh leaving each with a pitch shot of a little over 100 yards to the green. Both players were to the right of the hole, Jones about eight feet away, Sommerville seven feet away. Bob gently stroked his right-to-left breaking putt, the ball momentarily hung on the upper edge of the hole, then tumbled in for a birdie three. Sandy barely missed. Jones went 2 up as this proved to be the critical hole in the match, as Jones prevailed 5 and 4.

In the afternoon match, Jones met Fred Hoblitzel, another Canadian. Bob defeated him by the same 5 and 4 score as he had Sommerville in the morning round. Several of the top players had fallen in the first round - Francis Ouimet, Johnny Goodman, Doc Willing and Philip Perkins. George Voigt and George Von Elm lost in the second round.

Finally the dreaded 18-hole matches, where anyone could get hot over a short stretch, were over. It was on to the comfort of the longer 36-hole matches.

In the Thursday quarterfinal match Jones got by Californian Fay Colemen by a score of 6 and 5.

When Jones sunk his putt on the 16th green in his match with Fay Coleman, he immediately conceded Coleman's putt for a half.

Bob Jones drives from the first hole.

Jones and Sommerville before their match.

THE SEMI-FINAL MATCHES

"In the semi-final match at Merion I had a match with Gene Homans and Jones had a match with his good friend Jess Sweetser. They went out first because they were in the top bracket. Jones got ahead of Sweetser right off and it didn't look like it was going to be too much of a match. As I recall he had gotten 67 in one of the rounds. 67 was far out of reach. It would be like shooting a 62 today. Bob ended up winning 9 and 8.

"As it turned out Homans did not one of his very good rounds when he played me in the first 18 and I went to lunch five up on him.

"At the time they had come out in the golf world with a new club—a concave face like a sand wedge. It was just like a cup where if you became adept with it, you could hit the ball out of the bunker and it would just go up and flop and not move. My dad was a USGA Committeeman at the time and he told me that he didn't think the club was legal and he suggested that I didn't use it.

"That afternoon Homans must have laid about five shots out of the bunkers and high rough with this club, which I certainly could have used but didn't because my dad didn't think I should. Homans shot 69 in the afternoon, I was maybe 77. I lost all five holes including the 18th.

"It never crossed my mind that if I had beaten Homans, I would be playing Bobby Jones the next day."

—*Charlie Seaver*

Editor's Note: At the time Charlie Seaver was a youngster of 19 about to enter his freshman year at Stanford University. Incidentally, he is the father of Hall of Fame pitcher Tom Seaver.

☞ The crowds at Merion set a record for the U.S. Open.

Tom Nieporte

THE FINAL

"Of course I went out and watched the final match. There was such a huge amount of people that they got the Marines out to herd Bob through the ropes and get to the tee, because people were grabbing at Jones and reaching out for him.

"During the final match against Jones Homans again played badly on the first 18 as he had against me. As I recall, Jones didn't play that well on the first nine but shot a 33 on the back to go into the clubhouse at lunch with a seven-up lead."

—*Charlie Seaver*

☞ Herbert Jacques (at Jones' right), a member of the USGA Executive Committee, escorts Jones during the final round at Merion.

Below: Large crowds following the historic final round match.

A CONCEDED PUTT

"On the 11th hole Jones hit two perfect shots.

"He was there even with or just beyond the hole about 12-14 feet away from the cup. Homans got on the green down below and had about a 25 foot putt. He hit it towards the hole and missed it. He didn't even walk over to his ball, he just walked towards Bobby and shook his hand. That was it. Homans just conceded.

"Bobby never even putted."

—*Charlie Seaver*

A plaque commemorating Jones' victory at Merion used to reside near the 11th green at Merion. It now is located in the Bob Jones Room at Golf House, the USGA's headquarters, in Far Hills, New Jersey.

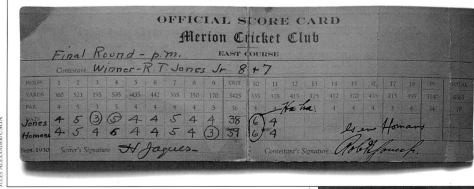

The final round scorecard.

☞ Homans concedes the match to Jones.

Grand Slam!

Incredibly, throughout the Amateur at Merion Bob Jones was never down to any opponent and was never really in any trouble. Although his play was not at the highest level the whole time, he did play well when he had to.

Bob Jones had accomplished the seemingly impossible. He had won all four of the major tournaments of the year - the British Amateur at St. Andrews, the British Open at Hoylake, the U.S. Open at Interlachen and now the U.S. Amateur at Merion.

It is safe to say that this is a record which will never be equaled. Certainly, it is a record that will never be broken.

Jules Alexander/Atlanta Athletic Club

The golf ball used by Jones in the final round at Merion.

Bob Jones receives the Havermeyer trophy at the conclusion of the U.S. Amateur.

NOVEMBER 1930

*F*OUNDED November, 1908, and published monthly. Devoted to the interests of golf and golfers, and the legitimate promotion of the game. Independent in its policies and not affiliated with any golf organization.

*T*HE aim of this publication is to aid in the development of golf and at the same time to help cultivate in devotees of the game a spirit of good sportsmanship and fair play for which golfers have long been noted.

The American Golfer

Untrod Ground

How One Man Finally Took the Uncertain Feature Out of a Seldom Certain Game

By Grantland Rice

THERE are two features of the recent amateur golf championship which blend together to make the final story. They show at last how Bobby Jones walked upon the untrod ground of a game always full of uncertainties and inconsistencies. The uncertainties of the game as applied to our leading stars could never be better shown than the results and aftermath of the qualifying rounds.

In the qualifying struggle Maurice McCarthy, Jr. had to make a hole in one to tie for the play-off and then face two play-off tests late Tuesday and early Wednesday. Yet after beating Watts Gunn in the morning, he eliminated George Von Elm in the afternoon, just after Von Elm had finished a forenoon round that was three or four under the par—one of the finest rounds in the tournament. For three weeks George Von Elm had been playing the finest golf of his life. Yet he passed out the first day.

Jack Ahern of Buffalo and Jess Sweetser of New York also finished in a tie for last place, whereupon Ahern came within an ace of eliminating Sweetser, carrying him to the nineteenth hole after Sweetser had dropped a forty-foot putt on the eighteenth green. Then Sweetser went on to the semi-finals.

Young Charlie Seaver of Los Angeles barely made the qualifying grade, yet he came within one hole of reaching the final round to face Bobby Jones at the wind-up. Doc Willing of Portland had been playing the best golf of his career, turning in one 70, yet he fell in the first round when Lawson Little fired a volley of five long putts from twenty to twenty-five feet.

Here you have the story of golf's uncertainties, showing how the best can suddenly step into the path of a tidal wave. A year ago this maelstrom caught Bobby Jones. But Johnny Goodman, the man who beat Jones last year, toppled out on the first round at Merion.

No Uncertainty Here

THE point is that in the midst of all these uncertainties Bobby Jones was never close to an uncertain turn. He almost gave the appearance of loafing through the championship, putting on pressure when he had to do so, but never crowding himself. Against Johnny Goodman at Pebble Beach he lost the first three holes where he started 5-6-4, two over par. Against Ross Somerville, a high grade golfer in his first start at Merion, Jones went out in 33 and finished the round 4 under par. There was no uncertainty about this match from the start.

You can understand how extended or extensive the uncertainties of golf are when you recall that Jimmy Johnston, the defending champion who won at Pebble Beach a year ago, failed to qualify—

That Doc Willing, who reached the final round at Pebble Beach lost in his first round—

That Chandler Egan, who reached the semi-final frame at Pebble Beach failed to qualify—

That Francis Ouimet fell in his first round against an eighteen-year-old entry from Detroit—

That Von Elm, Willing, Voigt failed to reach the thirty-six hole test.

That Don Moe, one of the finest players in the field, failed to qualify—

That Roland McKenzie who had been playing brilliant-

ly before the tournament, failed to qualify—

These are just a few cases. Apparently something of a highly harassing nature was happening to every star in the field—except Bobby Jones. When you consider all this and figure that Jones started at Sandwich last May in the Walker Cup matches, and never lost a match through the closing days of September at Merion—with two medal play victories over the finest professionals in the game, you can see just what is meant by the one man who at last was able to lift himself above the uncertainties and inconsistencies of a game, that at one time or another takes them all by the throat and leaves them throttled on the field. It has taken Bobby Jones by the throat more than once—but through his famous five-month campaign of 1930 he was at last able to shake himself loose from the grim grip that marks the game.

About This Record

JUST consider these cold and unbiased facts—

Starting early last April in the Southeastern Open at Augusta, Bobby Jones led a field of crack professionals including Horton Smith, Gene Sarazen, Johnny Farrell, Al Espinoza, Ed Dudley and many others by thirteen strokes in seventy-two holes of medal play.

He led a fine field at Hoylake in seventy-two holes through the British Open.

He led a stronger field at Interlachen through seventy-two holes in the U.S. Open.

He led the amateurs through thirty-six holes of medal play at Merion. Here you have a test of two hundred and fifty-two holes at medal play against the finest professionals and amateurs in golf on both sides of the Atlantic where Jones finished in front at every start.

What about match play?

Jones won his match at Sandwich in the Walker Cup play. He won eight matches in the British Amateur. He won five matches in the U.S. Amateur, making a total of thirteen matches, most of them over the shorter eighteen-hole route, where almost anything can happen.

When you consider these two records at medal and match play and recall again how quickly golfing form and the touch of the game can grow sour and stale, you begin to get a better idea of the job he handled through this season, through the almost endless strain that started at Augusta and then ran through Sandwich, St. Andrews, Hoylake, Interlachen and Merion.

In any other game, this record might not be listed as such an outstanding feat. In tennis, for example, if you can beat an opponent somewhat decisively one day you can beat him the next day—or next month. Form and touch and timing don't vary so suddenly. There are exceptions, but they are wide apart, although the last tennis season broke a record in this respect.

But golf is a different sort of game. It comes and goes. Even with Tommy Armour's wonderful 1930 record he lost his touch at Interlachen after opening with a 70. Even the smooth swinging Mac Smith had one or two off days in tournament play. The records of Armour and Smith were phenomenal. In some respects they reached even more brilliant heights, at their best, than anything golf ever knew before. And in his final stand where the strain is usually the hardest there was almost no contest. It was a week of slaughter.

The answer to this might be explained in these few words—

1. The correct fundamentals of swinging—perfect balance, body turn, head and hand action.

2. Ability to handle almost unlimited concentration through the grind.

3. Unusual determination that is proof against discouragement.

4. Exceptional physical strength and stamina.

5. The experience of twenty-eight major championships.

This was the combination that turned the trick. To this, one must add a blend of genius that is always beyond diagnosis—that has no place in any clinic. The results are obtained with an ease and grace that are not to be developed, unless they were born in the system. Of the thousands of pictures taken of Bobby Jones, no one can recall an awkward pose, an awkward swing, a sign of effort beyond control.

One of the features of this championship was the play of the young stars—Charlie Seaver, Fay Coleman, Lawson Little and Johnny McHugh from the Pacific coast—Charles Kocsis of Detroit—Sidney Noyes of New York, and several others. They put out such veterans as Willing, Von Elm, Voigt and Ouimet and gave promise of future fame.

Seaver showed to the best advantage among the youngsters, of course, where only a great par-equalling rally by Homans in the afternoon round stopped him from forging his way into the final by a single hole. This broad-shouldered, blond-thatched youngster, who may before long be making gridiron history with Pop Warner's Stanford football team, created a very favorable impression indeed. He is a tremendous hitter, certainly one of the longest in the field, both with wood and iron clubs. He still lacks something in his short game, but he is sure to do big things in coming years.

Sidney Noyes of New York and Charles Kocsis, the latter a high school boy of Detroit, were among the youngest players in the field, yet both of them played brilliant golf. Noyes turned in a round of 70 in his first start in the qualifying test, while Kocsis carded a 72 in his second start to reach a tie for seventh place in the list. Then by way of proving that this preliminary performance was no fluke, he shot a par 36 at Francis Ouimet over the first nine holes of their match to pick up a lead which the veteran was unable to overcome. In the afternoon round, he skidded and fell a victim to Bill McPhail, who incidentally had to go nineteen holes to stop Noyes in the morning. Coleman, Little and McHugh all qualified at Pebble Beach last year.

There were several others of the young school, including Leonard Martin of New York, Johnny De Paolo of Los Angeles, Charlie Mayo, Jr. of New York, Eddie Hogan of Portland and Sam Perry of Birmingham who miss out in the qualifying round by very thin margins, either of whom would have made the select circle with a favorable break here and there. Never was there a stronger field of youngsters coming along ready to step in and replace the veterans than there is just now.

The Merion Cricket Club did itself proud in handling the championship. Rarely has there been a gallery better behaved and directed, even though some fifteen thousand or more were on hand for the final match on Saturday, each intent on seeing as much as he or she could of Bobby Jones' history-making performance. The course showed the results of the unlimited care and preparation which had been spent on it to have it in the best possible condition.

"He combined exquisite artistry with utterly relentless precision in a way not quite given to other golfers. ..."
— Bernard Darwin

"Jones accomplished his prodigies of shotmaking with what was far and away the best swing of his time — and one of the best swings of all time." — Herbert Warren Wind

BY BEN CRENSHAW

B ob Jones' swing is characterized by a few things: first, he had a narrow stance, narrower than any champion before or since, which permitted a free hip turn; he was totally relaxed over the ball and he gripped the club very lightly. His left side dominated his swing with the right coming in just at impact.

His swing portrays rhythm, balance, movement and power like no other swing I ever saw. It's just the most rare, beautiful movement. It is beautifully simple. It is such a clean swing.

1

Although you can not see it here, he started his swing with a beautiful and very natural forward press with the

2

hands accompanied by a slight movement with his right knee. Note the narrowness of his stance.

3

He then let his left arm guide the start of the club going back, the right hand is barely holding on. This actually started

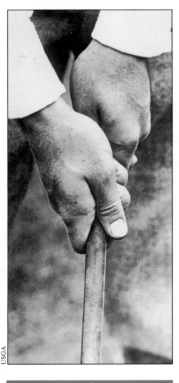

USGA

THE BETTMANN ARCHIVE

GRIP

◀ Jones had a magnificent grip. It almost looked like his hands were made to hold a golf club. He employed a Vardon overlapping grip. It's no wonder - at age 11 young Bob saw Vardon play an exhibition match at East Lake and in 1920 was paired with Vardon in the U.S. Open at Inverness.

FULL SWING STOP-ACTION

▼ "Jones' swing, one might say, was done in waltz time and merely to see it brought joy to the beholder." — *Al Laney*

THE BETTMANN ARCHIVE

FULL SWING

"Bob had an absolutely beautiful golf swing. It was just so fluid and easy. It was just perfect.

"He was confident that he could do what he was trying to do with a golf ball and could extend the distance if he tried to. He didn't really try to hit the ball a mile past everyone else. He would just be content to get the ball out there in play.

"One day we were playing the long second hole at Riviera and the wind was up. My good friend from Stanford and I were both out in the fairway a good 220-225 yards from the green and into the wind. We both hit our brassies real well and couldn't get to the green. Bobby was just ahead of us in the right rough. I'll never forget it — he took out his driver and hit it out of the rough, just like a shot, and put the ball about 15 feet directly behind the hole!

"That showed us that if he wanted to, he could out hit us by 30 yards. To him the name of the game was consistency." — *Charlie Seaver*

ASSOCIATED PRESS

SETUP

▲ Bob played the ball pretty far up in his stance. He played it off his left toe/instep, thereby feeling he could stay behind the ball throughout his swing. His actual build, his rather large legs, ankles and trunk enabled him to be very steady over the ball. There was a lot of mass in his trunk and it gave him an extremely solid foundation with which to swing around his body. ▶

◀ (Editor's Note: The photograph taken on this page and the inset on the third page of this section were taken in 1940 by Professor Edgerton of MIT, an early pioneer in the use of stop-action photography. The picture on this page was taken at 1/100,000 of a second at 1/10,000 of a second intervals.)

| 4 | 5 | 6 | 7 | 8 |

a mismotion — a loop and a lag that is very evident here.

He liked to quote Abe Mitchell, one of the old British professionals, who said "a player must be able to move freely beneath himself". This meant that one should be active from the waist down. In other words, your hips, legs, ankles, and feet should be lively, not static.

Jones often talked about how he felt like he was leaving his hands at the top of the swing, then moving from the bottom

BACK SWING

▲ Bob believed strongly that the left arm guides the swing. He kept the right hand and right arm passive. He believed in a fairly straight left arm - not rigid, not immobile, but fairly firm.

He always said set the arc of the swing with the left arm and let the right follow. It is very evident that the right was always subdued until the last moment.

9

10

11

12

13

Notice how the club moves only a little from frame 8 to frame 10, yet the hips have almost totally unwound.

Bob Jones developed his "Carnoustie" swing by watching and then mimicking his teacher Stewart Maiden. Notice how

stationary his head is throughout the swing. His was a stationary swing but it still moved; it was a rotary motion. He

liked to call it "a well rounded swing", meaning his hands never got really high in the swing.

Note how the right hand is subdued until the very last instant.

DOWN SWING

◄ "In the wooden shaft era, because of the inherent torque and torsion of the clubs, all golfers worked on being smooth and not rushing their swing, since a minute flaw in timing might be magnified into a disastrous error, but no one was close to Jones when it came to executing the correct movements rhythmically, fluidly — almost lyrically.

"... Jones was a man of only medium size, but because of the fullness of his arc, his excellent balance, and his extraordinary timing he was one of the longest hitters of his day and quite possibly the finest wooden-club player ever.

"His shots had a distinctive flight, much higher than most golfers'. I remember standing with a group that included Walter Hagen behind a green on the Meadowbrook course, near Detroit, during the 1955 P.G.A. Championship, when Jack Burke, Jr., hit a towering 5-iron approach that was dead on line and coasted down right over the top of the flagstick. "That's how Jones's irons used to look," Hagen said. "The ball came in as big as a grapefruit."

"Jones understood the dynamics of the golf swing exceedingly well, and he knew what he was doing every step of the way."
— *Herbert Warren Wind*

| 14 | 15 | 16 | 17 | 18 |

Golf Illustrated (UK)

This is what the old teachers used to call "hitting past your chin". There is no question that Jones looked at the

ball mostly with his left eye (See photo inset below.). It certainly enabled him to really turn. If you can look at the ball

with your left eye, you can really turn. If you are right eye dominant and look at the ball at address with the right eye,

you can not turn as far back as you can the other way.

Simply magnificent balance — the result of doing everything correctly.

The Jones Family

The Bettmann Archive

IMPACT

▶ At impact he envisioned the left arm as sort of serving and the right hand as cracking a whip,

with the right subdued until the very last moment. Note how solid the left side is to hit against both

just prior to impact (photo number 13 in the swing sequence) and at impact (large photo above).

FINISH

The Jones Family

▲ I've never seen a prettier finish in anyone's golf swing. A good finish is always, always the final result of doing something

properly throughout the swing. It reflects balance and proper weight distribution throughout the swing. His finish is just perfect.

"I don't think the present generation has any idea of how wonderful Bob was on the greens. His lovely smooth stroke on his long approach putts left him with little kick-ins time after time. He had a superb sense of distance." — Gene Sarazen

"On the greens, he was a lovely putter. ... in a critical situation he never missed a short one." — Herbert Warren Wind

"In 1921, Bobby (utilized) more of the 'caddy-boy' method, rather lacking in smoothness and not holding out promise of steadiness. He changed all of that afterwards, and now his putting is surely the most perfect example of rhythm that was ever seen. ... it has been the consistent goodness of his putting that, more than anything else, has accounted for his victories." — Bernard Darwin

PUTTING

BY BEN CRENSHAW

ob Jones' putting stroke was a miniature of his full swing. Nothing is really different except the length of his backswing. In the Warner Brothers films he urges us to forget about immobility in the putting stroke. He actually encourages movement in the knees—especially with longer putts. He felt that it promotes smoothness in your stroke and it has a tendency to iron your stroke out. Rigidity does not produce a smooth stroke.

Although early in his career Jones putted with his feet—and especially his heels — close together; by the later part of the 1920's and his Grand Slam year of 1930, he was putting with his heels just about touching. I like looking at his later method with his heels together because there is such an absence of strain. And, of course, it was with this method he achieved his greatest success.

His putting stroke was so rhythmic and smooth—he truly let the clubhead swing when he putted. He had such a long beautiful stroke — he likened it to a sweeping motion. Bob felt that a short jabbing stroke did not have any smoothness or stability. He said the correct stroke requires the ability to judge a ball against the slope and try to achieve the proper pace. There's really nothing more to it. And that's exactly what I try to do.

THE "EARLY" SETUP

▶ In this photo, taken in the early part of his career, Bob's putting was not nearly as consistent as it was when he stood with his heels closer together. Note how much more bent over he is here than in the above photo.

In the early days Bob tried a lot of different stances — including setting-up closed to the hole, before settling in on the comfortable look we see in his Grand Slam days.

The development of his putting style went against the norm. Usually, good putters start off as good putters; Bob Jones went from being a sporadic putter to a great putter, very clearly one of the very best ever.

THE "GRAND SLAM" SETUP

▲ Notice how Bob stood slightly open to the hole and how his hands are set in front of the putter blade. He looked entirely natural and comfortable over the ball and he exhibits beautiful balance. It almost looks like he is setting up for a chip shot or a little pitch-and-run.

Bob's method was very straight forward: he lined up his putt, placed the blade in front of the ball, then behind it and then started his stroke — all done in one continuous movement. There was no stopping, as he kept in motion the whole time.

THE "GRAND SLAM" STROKE

▲ Note how the putter blade never passes his hands at the conclusion of his putting stroke. Also, how he stays down through the stroke.

A DILEMMA

While at the U.S. Amateur at Merion Bob Jones was approached concerning the production of a series of instructional films on golf. Although he declined to discuss it at the Amateur, when he arrived home in Atlanta he was contacted again. Jones liked the concept for several reasons: he felt he could help people with their golf games, it was a way to stay involved with the game and lastly, the financial arrangements were attractive.

However, the production of these films proved to be quite a dilemma for Jones. Since 1927 he had been writing a syndicated newspaper column on golf. The USGA ruled that this did not violate his amateur status since he wrote the columns himself.

The instructional films proved to be a thornier problem. Although he thought that there was not much difference between the written word and a film, he also realized that there was not much difference between giving a lesson on the tee and on celluloid.

As always, Jones was forthright about his intentions. He clearly felt that the making of these films would be against the spirit of the rules of amateur competition. Rather than cause a problem for the USGA, Bob choose to retire from active competition.

Top: Jones reviews the "dailies" along with film star Ben Lyon, film director George Marshal and actress Bebe Daniels, Lyon's wife.

Above: Jones on the tee as George Marshal directs the action.

On the set with the film crew. O.B. Keeler is seated writing the script

"HOW I PLAY GOLF"

The filming of the twelve short films entitled, *How I Play Golf*, began in Hollywood in March of 1931. Because of Jones' popularity, many Hollywood film stars volunteered to appear in the films at no cost to Warner Brothers. Among these were such notables as W.C. Fields, Loretta Young, Harold Lloyd, Joe E. Brown, Walter Huston, Richard Barthelmess, Leon Earl and Guy Kibee.

Each of the shorts developed around a loose story line and theme with Jones' golf lesson worked in. Much of the dialog was ad lib. To this day these short films are classics, not only for the golf lessons, but for the entertainment value as well.

ATLANTA HISTORY CENTER

SPECIAL COLLECTIONS DEPARTMENT, R.W. WOODRUFF LIBRARY, EMORY UNIVERSITY

Top: Bob gives a lesson to opera star Lucrecia Borgia.

Above: The film crew used in the production of the instructional films.

Right: Jones with film star Harold Lloyd.

☞ Comedian Joe E. Brown with Bob Jones.

THE BETTMANN ARCHIVE

THE 1936 VISIT TO ST. ANDREWS

On a trip to the Berlin Olympic Games of 1936 with Grantland Rice and Robert Woodruff (of Coca-Cola) and their wives, they stopped off at the golf resort at Gleneagles, Scotland.

Bob remarked that it would be a shame not to pay a visit to St. Andrews since they were so close. Rice called ahead to arrange a tee time.

What happened next was one of those sublime incidents in sports.

When they arrived at the Old Course, they were astonished to find 2,000 people awaiting Jones' arrival on the first tee. More were reported on the course in anticipation of Jones' round. Shop keepers in St. Andrews closed their stores to welcome their champion back. Several stores had signs in the front window that read "Closed. Our Bobby's Back."

It certainly was one of the most moving and spontaneous outpourings of affection and admiration from one to another. Bob Jones had come to the home of golf, and St. Andrews welcomed home their returning son.

Top and Above: Children, and adults too, wanted Jones' autograph.

☞ Getting set to tee off at the first hole at the Old Course, Bob is joined by Gordon Lockhart, Willie Auchterlone and the Captain of the Royal and Ancient.

The Freedom Of The City Award

ob Jones was selected as Captain of the inaugural American team for the World Amateur Golf Team Championship for the Eisenhower trophy, to be played in October of 1958 on the Old Course at St. Anderws.

About a month before the event was to take place, Jones received a cable from the Town Clerk of St. Andrews asking if he would accept the Freedom of the City when he came to St. Andrews the next month. Bob, thinking this was a simple presentation akin to receiving the keys to the city, wired his acceptance and gave it no further thought.

When he received a return cable from the Provost (mayor) of St. Andrews stating that preparations for the event were well under way, Jones began to get an inkling of the magnitude of the event. When he finally arrived in St. Andrews and the Town Clerk asked for a copy of his speech, Jones began to realize the full impact of the award. Although he said that he did not have a copy of his speech, he felt that he would find the right words when the time came at the awards ceremony.

On October 9, 1958 in the Younger Graduation Hall of St. Andrews University the Provost conferred on Jones the Freedom of the City not only for his achievements in golf alone but because he is "... a man of outstanding character, courage and accomplishment ...". Officially this honor conferred on Jones " ... the right to take divots on the Old Course, to chase rabbits there and to dry his laundry on the first and eighteenth fairways". However, the Provost described the true meaning of the award "... that he is free to feel at home in St. Andrews as truly in his first home of Atlanta ..." Bob Jones was the first American so honored in almost 200 years; the previous recipient was Benjamin Franklin in 1759.

In a moving ten minute speech Bob Jones said of the Old Course, "The more you study it, the more you love it, and the more you love it, the more you study it."; of the friendship of the people of St. Andrews, "You people have a sensitivity and an ability to extend cordiality in ingenious ways; and of his experiences at St. Andrews, I could take everything out of my life except my experiences at St. Andrews and I'd still have a rich, full life".

At the end of his speech, Bob left the stage and got into the electric golf cart that was provided him. Those assembled simultaneously broke into the old Scottish song, "Will Ye No Come Back Again". As Herb Wind observed after attending the ceremony, "So honestly heartfelt was this reunion for Bobby Jones and the people of St. Andrews (and for everyone) that it was ten minutes before many who attended were able to speak again in a tranquil voice."

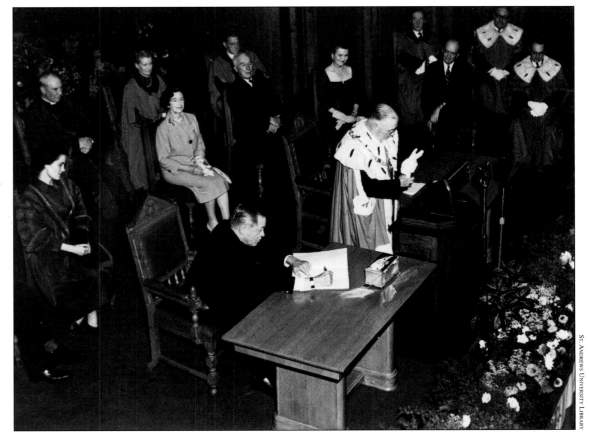

Left and Above: Bob Jones receives the Freedom of the City award of St. Andrews.

"... THE GREATEST GOLF SHOT I HAVE EVER SEEN"

— Bob Jones

ob Jones carefully counseled his players on how to play the Old Course, especially the critical — and tremendously difficult 17th. Based on Jones' knowledge and experience — remember the Road Hole was pivotal in several of his matches in the 1930 British Amateur, it was decided that no one would try to reach the 17th in two shots, but rather lay-up with the second and play the third as a short pitch shot to the green.

Amateur Bill Hyndman was selected to be the fourth and final player out on the course for the American side on the last day of competition. The weather was brutal - stiff winds accompanied by low temperatures. Playing well through 16 holes, Hyndman hit an excellent drive on the 17th hole and was left with a four iron into the green. He went up to Jones, who had driven his cart over to watch Hyndman, and said, "Bobby, I'm going to go for it." Jones, realizing that Hyndman needed to play the last two holes in one-under par to force a playoff with the Australian team, nodded his approval. Hyndman hit his shot with just enough fade to hold it against the right to left wind and the ball landed on the front edge of the upper terrace of the hard green, skipped by the pin and ended-up eight feet from the hole. At first glance Bill thought that the putt should be played just outside the left edge of the cup, but his caddy Little Mac (Dai Reece's caddy), an old St. Andrews hand who knew the course well, told him to play it for the center of the cup. Hyndman stroked it firmly—just where his caddy indicated and made the putt

for his 3. He went on to par the last to force a playoff.

Although the American team lost the playoff with the Australians the next day, Bill Hyndman's heroic effort on the 17th was duly noted. When Bill returned home to Philadelphia, he received a large framed picture of the Road Hole with a simple inscription, "This is the 17th hole at St. Andrews where Bill Hyndman hit the greatest golf shot I have ever seen." It was signed Bob Jones.

Top Right: Wherever Jones went at St. Andrews, the Scots expressed their admiration.

Above: Bill Hyndman drives off the tee during the World Team Amateur Chamionship.

Action on the Old Course during the World Team.

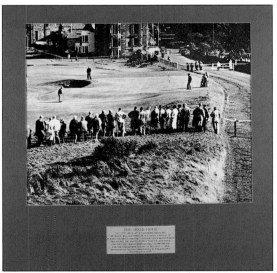

The framed picture Bill Hyndman recieved from Bob Jones when he returned home after the inaugural World Team.

A TRIBUTE

A memorial service of thanksgiving and commemoration was held for Bob Jones on May 4, 1972 at the Parish Church of the Holy Trinity Church in St. Andrews. Golf officials from around the world attended the service and tribute.

Pat Ward-Thomas of *The Manchester Guardian* described the solemn event:

"Twelve captains of the Royal and Ancient headed a goodly assembly of members, and the senior of them, Roger Wethered, gave the address. This was also fitting because Wethered played many times against Jones in the Walker Cup and in the 1930 final at St. Andrews. He had also taken part with Jones in the match at Hoylake in 1921 that led to the birth of the Walker Cup.

"Wethered spoke of seeing Jones, then 18, for the first time in 1920; and in paying tribute to his wonderful rhythm suggested that this helped his (Wethered's) sister, Joyce, to fulfill her own incomparable skill. He spoke also of the exceptional qualities of mind and character, which set Jones apart from other great players of games, and of his courage and dignity. Shortly before he died Jones said, "If this is the way it is, it sure is peaceful," and one rejoiced to know that he had found peace after all the years of suffering.

"The service was beautifully presented with a splendid choir and as we walked back from the church, sunlight filtered down upon the Old Course which Jones graced as no other man has done so many years ago. The bay sparkled silver in the breeze; it was a lovely golfing day he would surely have enjoyed even though he would not have approved of the richness of the turf and the slowness of the green. There in the club was the hickory driver he used in winning all four championships in 1930. As his son said: "You could go out and play with it now." It was a peaceful, gently memorable time, the like of which most of us will not know again.

"It was fitting then," Henry Longhurst of *The Sunday Times* wrote, "that if a memorial service should be held to perhaps the greatest golfer of all time, Bobby Jones, it should be held at St. Andrews."

Above: In addition to the Provost of St. Andrews and officials of the Royal and Ancient, Joe Dey, former Executive Director of the USGA and the first Commissioner of the PGA Tour (Back row, far right) attended the service.

The procession with the Captain's putter leading the way.

"Perhaps it is best simply to say that just as there was a touch of poetry to his golf, so there was always a certain, definite magic about the man himself."

— *Herbert Warren Wind*

THE COMPLETE RECORD OF ROBERT TYRE JONES, JR.

"His record represents the most consistently high competitive performance in the history of golf, if not any game."

— Al Laney

BY SALVATORE JOHNSON

■ **1902**
Born in Atlanta on St. Patrick's Day (March 17th).

■ **1907** (age 5)
Stricken in succession with whopping cough and measles. His parents brought Jones to a suburb of Atlanta and he played his first golf on a makeshift course at Frank Meador's house adjoining the East Lake course of the Atlanta Athletic Club.

■ **1908** (age 6)
EAST LAKE CHILDREN'S TOURNAMENT
Won by defeating Alexa Stirling, who would go on to win three U.S. Women's Amateur titles, Frank Meador and Perry Adair.

JUNIOR HANDICAP MATCH
Won tournament at match play, defeating Perry Adair in 36-hole final, 2 and 1. (Adair gave him a shot per hole.)

■ **1911** (age 9)
JUNIOR CHAMPIONSHIP CUP OF THE ATLANTA ATHLETIC CLUB
Won by defeating Howard Thorne, then 16 years old, 5 and 4 in 36-hole final.

■ **1912** (age 10)
ATLANTA ATHLETIC CLUB JUNIOR CHAMPIONSHIP
Lost to Howard Thorne in the semifinal. Thorne then lost to Perry Adair in the final.

■ **1913** (age 11)
EAST LAKE
Jones saw Harry Vardon and Ted Ray play an exhibition against Stewart Maiden and Willie Mann at East Lake and another the next day at Brookhaven. Jones observed that Vardon appeared to be playing an invisible opponent and was impressed by his steady scores: 72-72-73-71. Jones deduced Vardon was playing against par. A little later, Jones tried this approach and shot his first 80 on the old East Lake course. The concept became a key feature of Jones' play.

■ **1915** (age 13)
SOUTHERN AMATEUR
The East Lake Course of the Atlanta Athletic Club
Jones named to four-man team representing Atlanta Athletic Club, and shot lowest score of team, an 83, only one stroke behind the leaders.

Jones, the youngest player in the 64-man field, was pitted against the oldest, Commodore Bryan Heard, who defeated Jones 2 and 1. The defeat placed Jones in the second flight, where he lost in the final to Frank Clarke, who shot a new amateur course record of 76 to defeat Jones by 2 and 1.

☐ Lost in final of the second flight, Montgomery Invitation.

☐ Won invitation tournament at Roebuck Springs, Birmingham. Defeated Perry Adair in second round, 2 and 1. Defeated Bill Badham, former Yale player, in final at 21st hole. This was Jones' first win in an organized tournament, his first important win.

☐ Won Davis and Freeman Cup at East Lake.

☐ Won East Lake club championship by defeating his father in final. Also won Druid Hills Club Championship, shot a 73 in the final.

■ **1916** (age 14)
GEORGIA AMATEUR
Brookhaven Country Club
Jones won by shooting 70 in afternoon round to defeat Perry Adair 2 and 1.

MONTGOMERY INVITATION
Lost to Perry Adair in semifinal of first flight. Jones shot 33 going out, Adair shot 33 on inward half to win 1 up.

U.S. AMATEUR (September 4-9)
Merion Cricket Club, Ardmore, Pennsylvania
☐ Jones qualified for match play with 74-89=163.
☐ William C. Fownes, Jr. (winner in 1910) was the medalist with 153.
☐ All matches were at 36 holes.
☐ In the first round, Jones defeated Eben M. Byers (1906 champion) 3 and 1.
☐ In the second round, Jones defeated Frank W. Dyer 4 and 2.
☐ In the quarterfinal, Robert Gardner (winner in 1909 and '15) defeated Jones 5 and 3.
Gardner went on to the final, losing to Chick Evans 4 and 3.

BIRMINGHAM COUNTRY CLUB INVITATION
Won.

CHEROKEE CLUB INVITATION
Won in Knoxville, Tennessee, Jones shot 73 in final round.

EAST LAKE INVITATION TOURNAMENT
Won, defeating Perry Adair in the final.

■ **1917** (age 15)
SOUTHERN AMATEUR
Roebuck Springs Country Club in Birmingham, Alabama
In the final against Louis Jacoby, Jones shot 76 in the morning to go 4 up, and went on to win by 6 and 4.

DRUID HILLS INVITATION
Lost to Louis Jacoby in the second round.

■ **1918** (age 16)
SOUTHERN AMATEUR
Wins for the second time.

RED CROSS MATCHES
Tours the country with Alexa Stirling, Elaine

THE MEDALS OF BOB JONES, JR.

From 1923 through 1930, Robert T. Jones, Jr. won 13 National Championships. He earned at least one every year during that period. Jones reached his pinnacle in 1930, achieving the Grand Slam, then consisting of the Open and Amateur Championships of Great Britain and the United States.

In addition to his Amateur and Open titles, he was a member of five Walker Cup teams, became the first recipient of the James E. Sullivan Memorial Award in 1930, and was named Captain of the United States team in the 1958 World Amateur Team Championship at St. Andrews.

On November 17th, 1930, Jones announced his retirement from competetive golf at age 28.

Rosenthal and Perry Adair.

WAR RELIEF MATCHES
*Held at Baltusrol, Englewood, Siwanoy and
Garden City*
□ Jones won three singles and two foursome, lost one
foursome with Perry Adair to Emmett French and Jack
Dowling.

■ 1919 (age 17)
YATES-GODE TOURNAMENT
The East Lake Course of the Atlanta Athletic Club
quarterfinalist

CANADIAN OPEN
Hamilton Golf Club, Ontario, Canada
Jones finished T-2nd at 294 with Jim Barnes and Carl
Keffer, 16 behind winner J. Douglas Edgar.

CANADIAN - AMERICAN MATCH (July 25)
Hamilton (Ont.) Golf Club
Jones, a member of the 10-man U.S. team defeated a
Canadian team, 10 to 3. The return match was held in
September of 1920 at Engineers Club, Roslyn, NY
with the U.S. winning 10 to 4.

SOUTHERN AMATEUR
*New Orleans Country Club, New Orleans,
Louisiana*
Semifinalist, losing to Nelson Whitney, 6 and 5.

WESTERN AMATEUR
*Sunset Hill Country Club in
St. Louis, Missouri*
Jones was defeated in first round by Ned Sawyer.

U.S. AMATEUR (August 16-23)
Oakmont Country Club, Oakmont, Pennsylvania
□ Jones qualified for match play with 81-78=159.
□ He was one stroke behind medalists S. Davidson
Herron, Jimmy Manion and Paul Tewkesbury.
□ All matches were at 36 holes.
□ In the first round, Jones defeated Jimmy Manion 3
and 2.
□ In the second round, Jones defeated Robert Gardner
5 and 4.
□ In the quarterfinal, Jones defeated Rudolf Knepper 3
and 2.
□ In the semifinal, Jones defeated William C. Fownes,
Jr. 5 and 3.
□ In the final, S. Davidson Herron (whose home course
was Oakmont) defeated Jones 5 and 4.

SOUTHERN OPEN
The East Lake course of the Atlanta Athletic Club
Jones shot 73-74-76-71=294 to finish 2nd, one behind
winner Jim Barnes.

EXHIBITION MATCH AT EAST LAKE
Jim Barnes and Leo Diegel defeated Jones and J.
Douglas Edgar on the 19th hole.

■ 1920 (age 18)
GEORGIA AMATEUR
Druid Hills Golf Club in Atlanta, Georgia
Jones is semifinalist, defeated by C.V. Rainwater 1 up.

DAVIS-FREEMAN TOURNAMENT
East Course at Atlanta Athletic Club
Jones won, defeated Richard Hickey in the final 4
and 2.

SOUTHERN AMATEUR
Held in Chattanooga, Tennessee
Jones won, defeated Ewing Watkins in the final 10
and 9.

EXHIBITION MATCH (September 18)
Morris County Golf Club, Convent, New Jersey
Jones and Chick Evans defeat Harry Vardon and Ted
Ray in a 36-hole exhibition match 10 and 9.

WESTERN AMATEUR
Memphis Country Club, Memphis, Tennessee
□ Jones was the medalist by eight strokes with rounds
of 69-70=139; setting new tournament record.
□ In the first round, Jones defeated Frank Crager, 6
and 5.
□ In the second round, Jones defeated George
McConnell, 2 up.
□ In the third round, Jones defeated Clarence Hubby,
12 and 11.
□ In the semifinal, Jones lost to Chick Evans, 1 up.

U.S. OPEN (August 12-13)
Inverness Club, Toledo, Ohio
In the qualifying Jones, at 18 the youngest competitor,
was paired with Harry Vardon, at 50 the oldest. Jones
shot 75-76.
□ Jones shot 78-74-70-77=299 and finished T-8th, four
behind winner Ted Ray who shot 295.

MORRIS COUNTY INVITATIONAL
Winner

U.S. AMATEUR (September 6-11)
Engineers' Country Club, Roslyn, New York

	1919	1920	1921	1922	1923	1924	1925	1926	1927	1928	1929	1930

U.S. OPEN
• Winner
• Runner Up

U.S. Amateur
• Winner
• Runner Up
• Semi Finals
• Medalist

Walker Cup

British Open
• Winner

British Amateur
• Winner

□ Jones was co-medalist with 79-75=154. He was tied with Fred Wright, but by defeating Wright in their quarterfinal match won the honor.

□ All matches were at 36 holes.

□ In the first round, Jones defeated J. Simpson Dean 5 and 4.

□ In the second round, Jones defeated F.W. Dyer 5 and 4.

□ In the quarterfinal, Jones defeated Fred Wright 5 and 4.

□ In the semifinal, Francis Ouimet (winner in 1914) defeated Jones 6 and 5.

□ In the final, Ouimet was defeated by Chick Evans 7 and 6.

SOUTHERN OPEN
The East Lake course of the Atlanta Athletic Club
Jones shot 78-78-74-74=304 and finished 2nd, two behind J. Douglas Edgar

EXHIBITION MATCH (September 19)
Englewood Golf Club, Englewood, New Jersey
Jones and Cyril Walker defeat Vardon and Ray in the morning 3 and 2, then Jones and Oswald Kirkby defeated Harry Vardon and Ted Ray in the afternoon 3 and 2.

■ 1921 (age 19)
May 22, Hoylake, England
In an informal match between the U.S. and Great Britain & Ireland, the predecessor of the Walker Cup Matches which began the next year, the U.S. won 9 to 3. In the foursome, Jones teamed with Chick Evans and they defeated Gordon Simpson and Mr. Jenkins 5 and 3; in the singles, Jones defeated Mr. DeMontmorency 4 and 3.

BRITISH AMATEUR (May 23-27)
Royal Liverpool Golf Club, Hoylake, England

□ In the first round, Jones defeated G.C. Manford 3 and 2.

□ In the second round, Jones defeated E.A. Hamlet 1 up.

□ In the third round, Jones defeated Robert Harris (who would win 1925 British Amateur) 6 and 5.

□ In the fourth round, Alan Graham defeated Jones 6 and 5.

□ Graham went to the final, but was defeated by Willie Hunter 12 and 11.

BRITISH OPEN (June 23-25)
The Old Course, St. Andrews, Scotland
Jones qualified on June 21st with rounds of 76-76 on the Eden Course of St. Andrews.
Jones shot 152 for the first 36 holes, but picked up after taking 46 on the first nine, then a six on the 10th and hitting his ball into a bunker at the par 3 11th hole. He took two to get out of the bunker, missed his first putt, then picked up. He continued to play, however, and scored an unofficial 72 for the final round.
The winner of the championship was Jock Hutchison, who defeated Roger Wethered in a 36-hole play-off.

U.S. OPEN (July 21-22)
Columbia Country Club, Chevy Chase, Maryland

□ Jones shot 77 in 18 hole qualifier and nearly did not qualify.

□ Jones shot 78-71-77-77=303 and finished 5th, 14 shots behind winner Jim Barnes who shot 289.

WESTERN OPEN
Oakwood Country Club, Cleveland Heights, Ohio

□ Jones tied with Joe Kirkwood for 4th place. Jones shot 295 after leading the field at the 36-hole mark with 69-70.

□ Walter Hagen won the tournament with 287.

U.S. AMATEUR (September 17-24)
St. Louis Country Club, Clayton, Missouri

□ Jones qualified for match play with 76-75=151.

□ Francis Ouimet was the medalist with 146.

□ All matches were at 36 holes.

□ In the first round, Jones defeated Clarence L. Wolff 12 and 11.

□ In the second round, Jones defeated Dr. Oscar F. Willing 9 and 8.

□ In the quarterfinal, Willie Hunter (1921 British Amateur Champion) defeated Jones 2 and 1.

□ Eventual champion was Jess P. Guilford who defeated Robert Gardner 7 and 6.

■ 1922 (age 20)
SOUTHERN AMATEUR
The East Lake Course of the Atlanta Athletic Club

□ Jones, Perry Adair and T.W. Palmer shared the medalist honor, shooting 75.

□ In the first round, Jones defeated W.G. Oehmig 6 and 5.

□ In the second round, Jones defeated D.T. McRitchie 8 and 7.

□ In the third round, Jones defeated Chasteen Harris 11 and 9.

□ In the semifinal, Jones defeated Chris Brinke 12 and 11.

□ In the final, Jones defeated Frank Godchaux 8 and 7.

For the 123 holes Jones played he was 10 under par and it was his final appearance in the Southern Amateur

U.S. OPEN (July 14-15)
Skokie Country Club, Glencoe, Illinois

□ Jones shot 72-76 on July 11th to qualify for the Open.

□ Jones shot 74-72-70-73=289 and finished T-2nd, one behind winner Gene Sarazen.

INAUGURAL WALKER CUP MATCHES
(August 28-29)
National Golf Links of America, Southampton, New York

□ In the first day foursome, Jones and Jess W. Sweetser defeated Willie B. Torrance and C.V.L. Hooman 3 and 2.

□ In the second day singles, Jones defeated Roger Wethered 3 and 2.

□ The United States won the matches 8 to 4 for Great Britain.

U.S. AMATEUR (September 2-9)
The Country Club, Brookline, Massachusetts

□ Jones qualified for match play with 72-73=145, one stroke behind medalist Jesse P. Guilford.

□ All matches were at 36 holes.

□ In the first round, Jones defeated James J. Beadle 3 and 1.

□ In the second round, Jones defeated Robert Gardner 3 and 2.

□ In the quarterfinal, Jones defeated William McPhail 4 and 3.

□ In the semifinal, Jess W. Sweetser defeated Jones 8 and 7. This was Jones' worst defeat at match-play.
In the final, Sweetser defeated Chick Evans 3 and 2.

□ September 16, shot 63 in friendly match at East Lake.

■ **1923** (age 21)
EXHIBITION MATCH
Atlanta, Georgia and Nashville, Tennessee
Jones and Perry Adair defeated Jock Hutchison and Frank Godchaux in a 72-hole match. Jones shot 69-69-69-71.

U.S. OPEN (July 13-15)
Inwood Country Club, Inwood, New York
□ Jones shot 77-79 on July 12th to qualify for the Open.
□ Jones shot 71-73-76-76=296 and finished tied with Bobby Cruickshank.
□ In the 18-hole play-off Jones shot 76 to win his first major championship.
□ Cruickshank shot 78.

EXHIBITION MATCH (September 12)
Westmoreland Country Club, Chicago, Illinois
The match was for the Japanese relief fund. Jones and Bob Gardner lost 1 down to Jock Hutchison and Bob MacDonald.

U.S. AMATEUR (September 15-22)
Flossmoor Country Club, Flossmoor, Illinois
□ Jones was co-medalist in the qualifying rounds with 75-74=149.
□ He was tied with Chick Evans and won medalist honors in a playoff, defeating Evans 72-76.
□ All matches were at 36 holes.
□ In the first round, Jones defeated Tom B. Cochran 2 and 1.
□ In the second round, Max Marston defeated Jones 2 and 1.
□ Marston went on to defeat Jess W. Sweetser for the title on the 38th hole.

■ **1924** (age 22)
U.S. OPEN (June 5-6)
Oakland Hills Country Club, Birmingham, Michigan
Jones did not have to qualify for the 1924 U.S. Open since he was the defending champion.
Jones shot 74-73-75-78=300 and finished 2nd, three behind winner Cyril Walker.

CHALLENGE MATCH
The East Lake Course of the Atlanta Athletic Club
Jones lost to Arthur Havers, the British Open Champion, by one stroke in a 36-hole challenge match. Jones, shot 78-71, Havers 76-72.

EXHIBITION MATCH
Held in Augusta, Georgia
□ Jones and Perry Adair lost to Arthur Havers and Jimmy Ockenden, the French Open champion, 5 and 4.
□ Havers shot 70 on the sand greens, Jones 75.

EXHIBITION MATCH
East Lake and Druid Hills
□ Jones and Cyril Tolley each shot 74 in first round at East Lake.
□ In the second round at Druid Hills, Tolley edged Jones, 71 to 72.
□ In another match, Tolley and Perry Adair defeated Jones and Tim Bradshaw 3 and 1.

EXHIBITION MATCH
Asheville, North Carolina
Jones and Francis Ouimet lost to George Duncan and Abe Mitchell in a 36 hole exhibition 2 and 1.

WALKER CUP MATCHES (September 12-13)
Garden City Golf Club, Garden City, New York
□ In the first day foursome, Michael Scott and Robert Scott, Jr. defeated Jones and William C. Fownes, Jr. 1 up. This was Jones' only defeat in Walker Cup play.
□ In the second day singles, Jones defeated Charles O. Hezlet 4 and 3.
□ The United States won the matches 9 to 3 for Great Britain.

U.S. AMATEUR (September 20-27)
Merion Cricket Club, Ardmore, Pennsylvania
□ Jones qualified for match play with 72-72=144, two strokes behind medalist D. Clarke Corkran.
□ All matches were at 36 holes.
□ In the first round, Jones defeated W.J. Thompson 6 and 5.
□ In the second round, Jones defeated D. Clarke Corkran 3 and 2.
□ In the quarterfinal, Jones defeated Rudolf Knepper 6 and 4.
□ In the semifinal, Jones defeated Francis Ouimet 11 and 10.
□ In the final, Jones defeated George Von Elm 9 and 8.

■ **1925** (age 23)
WEST COAST OF FLORIDA OPEN
St. Petersburg, Florida
Jones shot 76-75-78-79=308, his worst performance in a stroke play event and finished in 16th place, 19 strokes behind the winner, Tommy Armour.

U.S. OPEN (June 3-5)
Worcester Country Club, Worcester, Massachusetts
□ Jones shot 71 on May 28 and then the next day shot 72 at the Lido Links to qualify for the U.S. Open. It would be the last time that Jones would have to qualify for the U.S. Open.

□ Jones shot 77-70-70-74=291 and finished tied with Willie MacFarlane. In the 36-hole play-off, MacFarlane shot 75-72 to defeat Jones by one. Jones scores were 75-73.

U.S. AMATEUR (August 31- September 5)
Oakmont Country Club, Oakmont, Pennsylvania
Jones qualified for match play with 75-72=147, two strokes behind medalist Roland MacKenzie.
□ All matches were at 36 holes. Only 16 players qualified for match play.
□ In the first round, Jones defeated William M. Reekie 11 and 10.
□ In the second round, Jones defeated Clarence L. Wolff 6 and 5.
□ In the semifinal, Jones defeated George Von Elm 7 and 6.
□ In the final, Jones defeated Watts Gunn 8 and 7 to win the championship for the second year in a row.

■ **1926** (age 24)
EXHIBITION MATCH
St. Petersburg, Florida
Jones and Tommy Armour defeated Walter Hagen and Gil Nicholls 4 and 3.

EXHIBITION MATCH
Sarasota, Florida
Jones and Tommy Armour defeated Arnaud Massy (1907 British Open Champion) and Archie Compston 8 and 7.

EXHIBITION MATCH
Sarasota, Florida
Jones and Armour defeated Gene Sarazen and Leo Diegel 3 and 2.

EXHIBITION MATCH
Sarasota and St. Petersburg, Florida
Jones lost to Walter Hagen in a special 72 hole match 12 and 11.

WEST COAST OF FLORIDA OPEN
St. Petersburg, Florida
Jones shot 75-69-71-70=285 and finished 2nd, two strokes behind winner Walter Hagen.

BRITISH AMATEUR
(May 24-29)
Muirfield Golf Club, Muirfield, Scotland
□ In the first round, Jones defeated Major C.B. Omerod 3 and 2.

□ In the second round, Jones defeated Colin C. Aylmer 6 and 4.

□ In the third round, Jones defeated Hugh M. Dickson 4 and 3.

□ In the fourth round, Jones defeated J. Birnie, Jr. 7 and 6.

□ In the fifth round, Jones defeated Robert Harris 8 and 6. The match was interesting because it pitted the defending British Amateur champion (Harris) and Jones, the defending U.S. Amateur champion.

□ In the sixth round, Andrew Jamieson, Jr. eliminated Jones by defeating him 4 and 3.

□ Eventual Champion was Jess Sweetser who defeated A.F. Simpson 6 and 5.

WALKER CUP MATCHES (June 2-3)
The Old Course,
St. Andrews, Scotland
☐ In the first day foursome, Jones and Watts Gunn defeated Cyril Tolley and Andrew Jamieson 4 and 3.
☐ In the second day singles, Jones defeated Cyril Tolley 12 and 11.
☐ The United States won the matches 6 to 5 for Great Britain.

EXHIBITION MATCH
Moor Park, England
Jones and Walter Hagen defeated Abe Mitchell and Cyril Tolley 4 and 2.

BRITISH OPEN (June 23-25)
Royal Lytham and St. Annes, Southport, England
☐ Jones shot 66-68=134 at Sunningdale Golf Club in England to lead the qualifying by seven strokes, setting a new record.
☐ Jones shot 72-72-73-74=291 to win by two strokes over Al Watrous, tying the British Open record.

U.S. OPEN (July 8-10)
Held at Scioto Country Club, Columbus, Ohio
Jones shot 70-79-71-73=293 to defeat Joe Turnesa by one. Jones birdied the 72nd hole for his second U.S. Open title.

U.S. AMATEUR (September 13-18)
Held at Baltusrol Golf Club, Springfield, New Jersey
☐ Jones was medalist by three strokes with 70-73=143.
☐ The first two rounds were at 18 holes, the others at 36.
☐ In the first round, Jones defeated Richard A. "Dickie" Jones 1 up.
☐ In the second round, Jones defeated William M. Reekie 5 and 4.
☐ In the third round, Jones defeated Chick Evans 3 and 2.
☐ In the semifinal, Jones defeated Francis Ouimet 5 and 4.
☐ In the final, George Von Elm defeated Jones 2 and 1.

■ **ENTERED EMORY UNIVERSITY LAW SCHOOL**

■ **1927** (age 25)
SOUTHERN OPEN
The East Lake Course of the Atlanta Athletic Club
Jones shot 72-66-71-72=281 and won by eight shots over Johnny Farrell.

U.S. OPEN (June 14-16)
Oakmont Country Club, Oakmont, Pennsylvania
Jones shot 76-77-79-77=309 to T-11th, eight behind winner Tommy Armour and his worst finish in the U.S. Open.

EXHIBITION MATCH
Epsom, England
Jones and Joe Kirkwood defeated Roger Wethered and Cyril Tolley 1 up.

BRITISH OPEN (July 13-15)
The Old Course, St. Andrews, Scotland
☐ Qualified with 76-71; 71 tied the 18-hole course record.
☐ Jones successfully defended his championship with rounds of 68-72-73-72=285, defeating Aubrey Boomer and Fred Robson by six strokes.

U.S. AMATEUR (August 22-27)
Minikahda Club, Minneapolis, Minnesota
☐ Jones was medalist by three strokes with 75-67=142.
☐ The first two rounds were at 18 holes, the others at 36.
☐ In the first round, Jones defeated Maurice J. McCarthy 2 up.
☐ In the second round, Jones defeated Eugene V. Homans 3 and 2.
☐ In the third round, Jones defeated Harrison R. Johnston 10 and 9.
☐ In the semifinal, Jones defeated Francis Ouimet 11 and 10.
☐ In the final, Jones defeated Chick Evans 8 and 7.

■ **1928**
U.S. OPEN (June 21-24)
Olympia Fields Country Club (No. 4 course), Matteson, Illinois
☐ Jones shot 73-71-73-77=294 and finished tied with Johnny Farrell.
☐ In the 36-hole play-off, Farrell shot 70-73 to defeat Jones by a stroke. Jones shot 73-71.

WARREN K. WOOD MEMORIAL
Held at Flossmoor Country Club, Flossmoor, Illinois
Jones shot 37-30=67, scoring seven 3s in succession to win the tournament.

☐ In warmups for the Walker Cup, Jones shot 69-71-69-68 at Biltmore Forest Country Club; at Old Elm he shot a course record of 68; at Chicago Golf Club he set new course record with a 68, then shot 67 on the following day, only to shoot a 68 on the third day.

WALKER CUP MATCHES (August 30-31)
Chicago Golf Club, Wheaton, Illinois
☐ In the first day foursome, Jones and Chick Evans defeated Charles Hezlet and William Hope 5 and 3.
☐ In the second day singles, Jones defeated R. Philip Perkins 13 and 12.
☐ The United States won the matches 11 to 1 for Great Britain.

EXHIBITION MATCH
Baltimore, Maryland
☐ Jones and Watts Gunn tied Roland MacKenzie and Warren Corkran.
☐ MacKenzie shot 74, Jones 77.

EXHIBITION MATCH
Woodland Golf Club, Newton, Massachusetts
Jones and Johnny Farrell lost to Walter Hagen and Gene Sarazen 1 up. Jones shot 69-67 in the match.

U.S. AMATEUR (September 10-15)
Brae Burn Country Club, West Newton, Massachusetts
☐ Jones qualified for match play with 77-74=151, eight strokes behind medalist George J. Voigt.
☐ The first two rounds were at 18 holes, the others at 36.
☐ In the first round, Jones defeated J.W. Brown 4 and 3.
☐ In the second round, Jones defeated Ray Gorton on

the 19th hole.
☐ In the third round, Jones defeated John B. Beck 14 and 13.
☐ In the semifinal, Jones defeated Phillips Finlay 13 and 12.
☐ In the final, Jones defeated T. Philip Perkins (1928 British Amateur Champion) 10 and 9.

☐ Passed Georgia bar exam after two years in law school.

■ **1929** (age 27)
U.S. OPEN
Winged Foot Golf Club (West Course), Mamaroneck, New York
Jones shot 69-75-71-79=294 and finished tied with Al Espinosa. In the 36-hole play-off, Jones shot 72-69=141 to defeat Espinosa by 23 strokes.

U.S. AMATEUR (September 2-7)
Pebble Beach Golf Links, Pebble Beach, California
☐ Jones was co-medalist in the qualifying rounds with 70-75=145.
☐ He was tied with Eugene V. Homans.
☐ The first two rounds were at 18 holes, the others at 36.
☐ In the first round, Johnny Goodman defeated Jones 1 up.
☐ Eventual Champion was Harrison R. Johnston who defeated Dr. Oscar F. Willing 4 and 3.
☐ After loss to Goodman, Jones played Cypress Point and fell in love with the course designed by Alister Mackenzie.

■ **1930** (age 28)
SAVANNAH OPEN
Savannah, Georgia
Jones shot 67-75-65-72=279 and finished second, one stroke behind winner Horton Smith.

SOUTHEASTERN OPEN
Augusta, Georgia
Jones shot 72-72-69-71=284 to win by 13 strokes over Horton Smith.

GOLF ILLUSTRATED GOLD VASE
Sunningdale, England
Jones shot 75-68=143 to win.

WALKER CUP MATCHES (May 15-16)
Royal St. George's Golf Club, Sandwich, England
☐ In the first day foursome, Jones and Dr. Oscar F. Willing defeated Rex W. Hartley and Thomas A. Torrance 8 and 7.
☐ In the second day singles, Jones defeated Roger Wethered 9 and 8.
☐ The United States won the matches 10 to 2 for Great Britain.

EXHIBITION MATCH
Oxhey, England
Jones shot 68 in a exhibition with Ted Ray, Harry Vardon, and James Braid.

BRITISH AMATEUR (May 26-31)
The Old Course, St. Andrews, Scotland
☐ The first round was a bye.
☐ In the second round, Jones defeated Sidney Roper 3 and 2.
☐ In the third round, Jones defeated Cowan

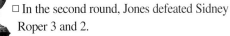

JULES ALEXANDER / USGA

Shankland 5 and 3.
□ In the fourth round, Jones defeated Cyril Tolley (1920 and '29 British Amateur Champion) on the 19th hole.
□ In the fifth round, Jones defeated G.O. Watt 7 and 6.
□ In the sixth round, Jones defeated Harrison R. Johnston (1929 U.S. Amateur Champion) 1 up.
□ In the seventh round, Jones defeated Eric Fiddian 4 and 3.
□ In the semifinal, Jones defeated George Voigt 1 up.
□ In the final, Jones defeated 1923 British Amateur champion Roger Wethered 7 and 6.

BRITISH OPEN
(June 18-20)
Royal Liverpool Golf Club, Hoylake, England
□ Jones qualified with a round of 73 at Hoylake on June 16 and a round of 77 at Wallasey on June 17.
□ Jones shot 70-72-74-75=291 to win his third British Open.
□ He defeated Macdonald Smith and Leo Diegel by two strokes.

U.S. OPEN (July 10-12)
Interlachen Country Club, Minneapolis, Minnesota
Jones shot 71-73-68-75=287 to win his 4th U.S. Open by two strokes over Macdonald Smith.

EXHIBITION MATCH
The East Lake Course of the Atlanta Athletic Club
Jones shot 70 before 3,000 fans in a benefit for the 82nd Division Entertainment Fund.

EXHIBITION MATCH
Columbia Country Club in Chevy Chase, Maryland
Jones and Roland R. MacKenzie defeated Macdonald Smith and Fred McLeod 1 up.

U.S. AMATEUR (September 22-27)
Merion Cricket Club, Ardmore, Pennsylvania
□ Jones was medalist by one stroke with 69-73=142.
□ The first two rounds were at 18 holes, the others at 36.
□ In the first round, Jones defeated C. Ross

Somerville 5 and 4.
□ In the second round, Jones defeated Fred G. Hoblitzel 5 and 4.
□ In the third round, Jones defeated Fay Coleman 6 and 5.
□ In the semifinal, Jones defeated Jess W. Sweetser 9 and 8.
□ In the final, Jones defeated Eugene V. Homans 8 and 7.

■ **1931** (age 29)
Began work on Augusta National with Alister Mackenzie as golf course architect.

■ **1932** (age 30)
Designed first set of matched irons for Spalding.

■ **1933** (age 31)
Augusta National completed and opened for play.

■ **1934** (age 32)
THE MASTERS
Augusta National Golf Club
Jones shot 76-74-72-72=294 and finished T-13th, 10 strokes behind winner Horton Smith

■ **1935** (age 33)
THE MASTERS
Augusta National Golf Club
Jones shot 74-72-73-78=297 and finished T-25th, 15 strokes behind winner Gene Sarazen.

EXHIBITION MATCH
The East Lake Course of the Atlanta Athletic Club
□ Jones and Dorothy Kirby tied Joyce Wethered and Charles Yates.
□ Jones shot a par 71, Wethered 74, Yates 76 and Kirby (who was then 15 years old) 84.

■ **1936** (age 34)
THE MASTERS
Augusta National Golf Club
□ Jones shot 78-78-73-77=306 and finished T-33rd, 21 strokes behind winner Horton Smith.

□ Jones shot 32-39=71 in an informal round at St. Andrews before 6,000 people.

■ **1937** (age 35)
THE MASTERS
Augusta National Golf Club
Jones shot 79-74-73-77=303 and finished T-29th, 20 strokes behind winner Byron Nelson.

■ **1938** (age 36)
THE MASTERS
Augusta National Golf Club
Jones shot 76-74-72-75=297 and finished T-16th, 12 strokes behind winner Henry Picard.

■ **1939** (age 37)
THE MASTERS
Augusta National Golf Club
Jones shot 76-77-78-73=303 and finished T-33rd, 25 strokes behind winner Ralph Guldahl.

■ **1940** (age 38)
THE MASTERS
Held at Augusta National Golf Club
Jones withdrew after two rounds.

■ **1941** (age 39)
THE MASTERS
Augusta National Golf Club
Jones shot 76-74-78-79=307 and finished 40th, 27 strokes behind winner Craig Wood.

CHALLENGE MATCH
Detroit Golf Club, Detroit Michigan
□ Jones captained a team of challengers which defeated the United States Ryder Cup side. Jones won his single from Henry Picard 2 and 1, but he and Gene Sarazen lost their foursome to Byron Nelson and Harold "Jug" McSpaden 8 and 6.

BAHAMAS RED CROSS EXHIBITION
Jones and Tommy Armour defeated Hagen and Sarazen 3 and 2.

□ Entered Army Air Corps although 4-F, with a commission as an intelligence officer.

□ Served for a while under Eisenhower.

■ **1942** (age 40)
THE MASTERS
Augusta National Golf Club
Jones shot 72-75-79-78=304 and finished T-29th, 24 strokes behind winner Byron Nelson.

HALE AMERICA NATIONAL OPEN (June 18-21)
Ridgemoor Country Club, Chicago, Illinois
□ Jones shot 70-75-72-73=290 to T-35th in a tournament that was the stand-in for the U.S. Open.
□ Ben Hogan won the event with 271.

■ **1946** (age 44)
THE MASTERS
Augusta National Golf Club
□ Jones shot 75-72-77-78=302 and finished T-32nd, 20 strokes behind winner Herman Keiser.
□ Jones played the first nine at East Lake in 29, six under.

■ **1947** (age 45)
THE MASTERS
Augusta National Golf Club
Jones shot 75-79-78-80=312 and finished 56th, 31 strokes behind winner Jimmy Demaret.

■ **1948** (age 46)
THE MASTERS
Augusta National Golf Club
Jones shot 76-81-79-79=315 and finished 49th, 36 strokes behind winner Claude Harmon.

□ Experiencing considerable pain in November, he underwent surgery at Emory to remove bone growths on three vertebrae.

■ **1955** (age 53)
Diagnosed with syringomyelia.

■ **1958** (age 56)
□ Awarded the Freedom of St. Andrews.
□ Non-playing captain of American team for inaugural World Team Amateur.

■ **1971** (age 69)
On December 18th, died in his sleep at home in Atlanta.

THE JONES RECORD IN MAJOR TOURNAMENTS

U.S. AMATEUR

■ **1916** — *Merion Cricket Club, Ardmore, Pa.*
1st round - defeated Eben M. Byers 3 and 1
2nd round - defeated Frank W. Dyer 4 and 2
quarterfinal - was defeated by Robert Gardner 5 and 3

■ **1919** — *Oakmont C.C., Oakmont, Pa.*
1st round - defeated Jimmy Manion 3 and 2
2nd round - defeated Robert Gardner 5 and 4
quarterfinal - defeated Rudolf Knepper 3 and 2
semifinal - defeated William C. Fownes, Jr. 5 and 3
final - was defeated by D. Davidson Herron 5 and 4

■ **1920** — *Engineers' C.C., Roslyn, N.Y.*
1st round - defeated J. Simpson Dean 5 and 4
2nd round - defeated F.W. Dyer 5 and 4
quarterfinal - defeated Fred Wright 5 and 4
semifinal - was defeated by Francis Ouimet 6 and 5

■ **1921** — *St. Louis C.C., Clayton, Mo.*
1st round - defeated Clarence L. Wolff 12 and 11
2nd round - defeated Dr. Oscar F. Willing 9 and 8
quarterfinal - was defeated by Willie Hunter 2 and 1

■ **1922** — *The Country Club, Brookline, Mass.*
1st round - defeated James J. Beadle 3 and 1
2nd round - defeated Robert Gardner 3 and 2
quarterfinal - defeated William McPhail 4 and 3
semifinal - was defeated by Jess W. Sweetser 8 and 7

■ **1923** — *Flossmoor C.C., Flossmoor, Ill.*
1st round - defeated Tom B. Cochran 2 and 1
2nd round - was defeated by Max Marston 2 and 1

■ **1924** — *Merion Cricket Club, Ardmore, Pa.*
1st round - defeated W.J. Thompson 6 and 5
2nd round - defeated D. Clarke Corkran 3 and 2.
quarterfinal - defeated Rudolf Knepper 6 and 4.
semifinal - defeated Francis Ouimet 11 and 10.
final - defeated George Von Elm 9 and 8

■ **1925** — *Oakmont C.C., Oakmont, Pa.*
1st round - defeated William M. Reekie 11 and 10
2nd round - defeated Clarence L. Wolff 6 and 5
semifinal - defeated George Von Elm 7 and 6
final - defeated Watts Gunn 8 and 7

■ **1926** — *Baltusrol Golf Club, Springfield, N.J.*
1st round - defeated Richard "Dickie" Jones 1 up
2nd round - defeated William M. Reekie 5 and 4
3rd round - defeated Chick Evans 3 and 2

semifinal - defeated Francis Ouimet 5 and 4
final - was defeated by George Von Elm 2 and 1

■ **1927** — *Minikahda Club, Minneapolis, Mn.*
1st round - defeated Maurice J. McCarthy 2 up
2nd round - defeated Eugene V. Homans 3 and 2
3rd round - defeated Harrison R. Johnston 10 and 9
semifinal - defeated Francis Ouimet 11 and 10
final - defeated Chick Evans 8 and 7

■ **1928** — *Brae Burn C.C., West Newton, Mass.*
1st round - defeated J.W. Brown 4 and 3
2nd round - defeated Ray Gorton 19th hole
3rd round - defeated John B. Beck 14 and 13
semifinal - defeated Phillips Finlay 13 and 12
final - defeated T. Philip Perkins 10 and 9

■ **1929** — *Pebble Beach G.L., Pebble Beach, Ca.*
1st round - was defeated by Johnny Goodman 1 up

■ **1930** — *Merion Cricket Club, Ardmore, Pa.*
1st round - defeated C. Ross Somerville 5 and 4
2nd round - defeated Fred G. Hoblitzel 5 and 4
3rd round - defeated Fay Coleman 6 and 5
semifinal - defeated Jess W. Sweetser 9 and 8
final - defeated Eugene V. Homans 8 and 7

IN THIRTEEN U.S. AMATEURS

☐ 51 matches played
☐ 43 wins 8 losses

☐ Matches that went to final hole: 10
☐ Won six of those matches

☐ In Jones' 13 U.S. Amateurs covering 51 matches, he played 37 different men, 10 of them more than once. He never lost to the same man twice. He won three of four matches from Francis Ouimet; two of three from George Von Elm and Robert Gardner; two each from Frank Dyer, Rudolf Knepper, Clarence Wolff, William Reekie, Chick Evans and Gene Homans; and divided two with Jess Sweetser.

■ **18 of Jones U.S. Amateur Records Still Stand Today**
☐ Most titles won: 5 (1924, '25, '27, '28 and '30)
☐ Most times appearing as finalist: 7 (1919, '24, '25, '26, '27, '28 and '30)
☐ Most times as finalist in successive years: 5 (1924, '25, '26, '27 and '28)

☐ Youngest quarter-finalist: was 14 at Merion in 1916
☐ Most times as medalist: 6 (1920, '23, '26, '27, '29 and '30) record tied with Walter Travis
☐ Lowest 18-hole score in qualifying rounds: 67 at Minikahda in 1927 - record tied with five others
☐ Never failed to qualify for the championship
☐ Best winning percentage in 20 or more matches: 84.3%
☐ Won his 43 matches by the average margin of 6.1 holes
☐ His eight loses were at the hands of national champions
☐ Most 36-hole matches won: 35
☐ Won his 35 matches at 36 holes by the average margin of 7 holes
☐ Most double-figure victories: 8
☐ Most double-figure victories in succession: 3 at Brae Burn in 1928
☐ Most double-figure victories in one championship: 3 at Brae Burn in 1928
☐ Largest margin of victory in a 36-hole match: 14 and 13 over John Beck at Brae Burn in 1928 (record shared with Jerome Travers
☐ Most hole up on opponents in one championship: 42 at Brae Burn in 1928
☐ In five matches, he had to play only 108 of a possible 144 holes
☐ He was 32 up on four opponents at Oakmont in 1925, playing only 116 of a possible 144 holes.

BRITISH AMATEUR

■ **1921** — *Royal Liverpool G.C., Hoylake, England*
1st round - defeated G.C. Manford 3 and 2
2nd round - defeated E.A. Hamlet 1 hole
3rd round - defeated Robert Harris 6 and 5
4th round - was defeated by Alan Graham 6 and 5

■ **1926** — *Muirfield G.C., Muirfield, Scotland*
1st round - defeated Major G.B. Ormerod 3 and 2
2nd round - defeated Colin C. Aylmer 5 and 4
3rd round - defeated Hugh M. Dickson 4 and 3
4th round - defeated J. Birnie Jr. 7 and 6
5th round - defeated Robert Harris 8 and 6
6th round - was defeated by Andrew Jamieson 4 and 3

■ **1930** — *Old Course, St. Andrews, Scotland*
1st round - bye
2nd round - defeated Sidney Roper 3 and 2
3rd round - defeated Cowan Shankland 4 and 3
4th round - defeated Cyril Tolley 19th hole
5th round - defeated G.O. Watt 7 and 6
6th round - defeated Harrison R. Johnston 1 hole
7th round - defeated Eric Fiddian 4 and 3
semifinal - defeated George Voigt 1 hole
final - defeated Roger Wethered 7 and 6

IN THREE BRITISH AMATEURS

☐ 18 matches played
☐ 16 wins 2 losses

☐ Matches that went to final hole: 4
☐ Won all 4 matches

☐ Match play record in U.S. Amateur and British Amateur
☐ 69 matches played
☐ 58 wins 11 losses

☐ Matches that went to final hole: 14
☐ Won all 10 matches

U.S. OPEN

Year	Place		Score	To Par	1st Rd	2nd Rd	3rd Rd	4th Rd	Play- off
1920	Inverness Club, Toledo, OH	T-8th	299	11	78	74	70	77	
1921	Columbia C.C., Chevy Chase, MD	T-5th	303	23	78	71	77	77	
1922	Skokie C.C., Glencoe, IL	T-2nd	289	9	74	72	70	73	
1923	Inwood C.C., Inwood, NY	Win	296	8	71	73	76	76	76
1924	Oakland Hills C.C., Birmingham, MI	2nd	300	12	74	73	75	78	
1925	Worcester C.C., Worcester, MA	2nd	291	7	77	70	70	74	148
1926	Scioto C.C., Columbus, OH	Win	293	5	70	79	71	73	
1927	Oakmont C.C., Oakmont, PA	T-11th	309	21	76	77	79	77	
1928	Olympia Fields C.C., Matteson, IL	2nd	294	10	73	71	73	77	144
1929	Winged Foot G.C., Mamaroneck, NY	Win	294	6	69	75	71	79	141
1930	Interlachen C.C., Minneapolis, MN	Win	287	-1	71	73	68	75	

U.S. Open Totals:	Strokes	Avg	1st	2nd	3rd	4th	Playoff
	3764	73.80	73.7	73.5	72.7	76.0	72.7

Jones participated in 11 U.S. Opens, playing 51 rounds of golf with a total of 111 strokes over par.
He finished in the Top 3 - 8 times, the Top 5 - 9 times, the Top 10 - 10 times, making 11 cuts.
Rounds in 60s: 2 Rounds under par: 11 Rounds at par: 3 Rounds over par: 37
Lowest Score in U.S. Open: 68 Highest Score in U.S. Open: 148

BRITISH OPEN

Year	Place		Score	1st Rd	2nd Rd	3rd Rd	4th Rd
1921	Old Course, St. Andrews, Scotland	Wd	152	78	74		
1926	Royal Lytham and St. Annes, Southport Eng	Win	291	72	72	73	74
1927	Old Course, St. Andrews, Scotland	Win	285	68	72	73	72
1930	Royal Liverpool G.C., Hoylake, Eng.	Win	291	70	72	74	75

Jones participated in 4 British Opens, playing 14 rounds of golf with a scoring average of 72.71.
He has finished in the Top 3 - 3 times, the Top 5 - 3 times, the Top 10 - 3 times, making 3 cuts.

WALKER CUP

■ **1922** — *National Golf Links of America, Southampton, N.Y.*
☐ 1st day foursome - Jones and Jess W. Sweetser defeated Willie B. Torrance and C.V.L. Hooman 3 and 2
☐ 2nd day singles - Jones defeated Roger Wethered 3 and 2
☐ The United States won the matches 8 to 4 for Great Britain

■ **1924** — *Garden City Golf Club, Garden City, N.Y.*
☐ 1st day foursome - Michael Scott and Robert Scott, Jr. defeated Jones and William C. Fownes, Jr. 1 up
☐ 2nd day singles -Jones defeated Charles O. Hezlet 4 and 3
☐ The United States won the matches 9 to 3 for Great Britain

■ **1926** — *Old Course, St. Andrews, Scotland*
☐ 1st day foursome - Jones and Watts Gunn defeated Cyril Tolley and Andrew Jamieson 4 and 3
☐ 2nd day singles - Jones defeated Cyril Tolley 12 and 11
☐ The United States won the matches 6 to 5 for Great Britain

■ **1928** — *Chicago Golf Club, Wheaton, Ill.*
☐ 1st day foursome - Jones and Chick Evans defeated Charles Hezlet and William Hope 5 and 3
☐ 2nd day singles - Jones defeated R. Philip Perkins 13 and 12
☐ The United States won the matches 11 to 1 for Great Britain

■ **1930** — *Royal St. George's Golf Club, Sandwich, England*
☐ 1st day foursome - Jones and Dr. Oscar F. Willing defeated Rex W. Hartley and Thomas A. Torrance 8 and 7
☐ 2nd day singles - Jones defeated Roger Wethered 9 and 8
☐ The United States won the matches 10 to 2 for Great Britain

All of the photographs in this section were taken at Golf House, the USGA's headquarters in Far Hills, New Jersey.

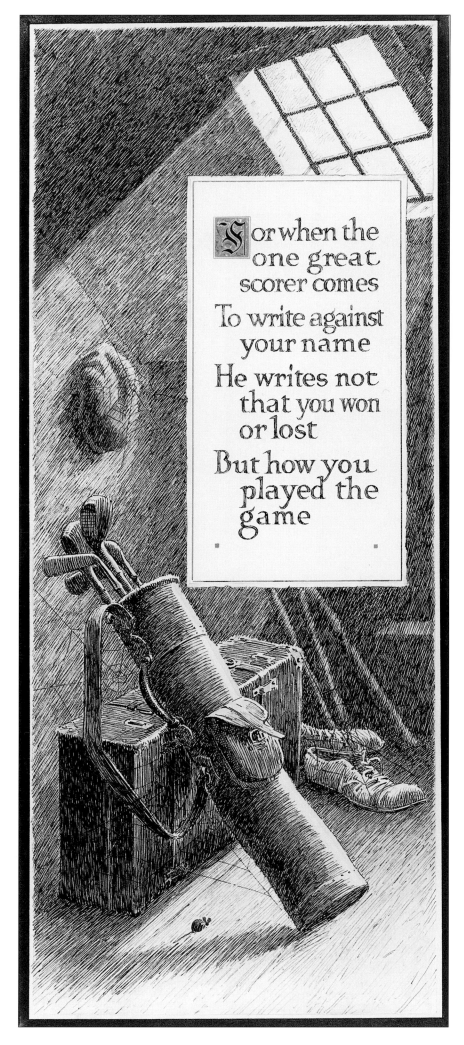

For when the
one great
scorer comes

To write against
your name

He writes not
that you won
or lost

But how you
played the
game

The framed quote by Grantland Rice that hung in Bob Jones' office.